A HISTORY OF THE
LONDON TAXICAB

G. N. Georgano

A HISTORY
of the
LONDON
TAXICAB

DAVID & CHARLES : NEWTON ABBOT

0 7153 5687 9

© G. N. GEORGANO 1972

Set in 11/13 Baskerville
and printed in Great Britain
by W J Holman Limited Dawlish
for David & Charles (Publishers) Limited
South Devon House Newton Abbot Devon

CONTENTS

CONTENTS

LIST OF ILLUSTRATIONS

PLATES

IN THE TEXT

FOREWORD

Among the many books published each year on motoring and transport history the taxicab has received scant attention. Lorry and bus enthusiasts tend to think of it as a private car, while motorists regard it as a commercial vehicle. Taxicabs may not have the glamour of racing cars, or the majesty of heavy goods and passenger vehicles, but they are used by almost everyone at one time or another, and Londoners are fortunate in having a purpose-designed vehicle which is not only interesting and unique but thoroughly practical as well. The London taxi is unusual in that it began as a light town car fitted with a meter, and has developed into a specialised machine, whereas foreign taxis have developed in precisely the opposite direction. Paris and Berlin had purpose-built taxis before the second world war, and the United States had at least half-a-dozen taxi-makers who built nothing else, but today London is alone in using a specialised taxi, apart from those provincial British cities which have London-type taxis as part of their fleets.

In this book I have tried to strike a balance between the development of cab design and the conditions of the cab trade, as each has influenced the other. I have dealt with the minicabs in some detail as they represent a serious threat to the traditional taxi, and one which has diminished not a bit for having become less blatant than in the early days of the Welbeck minicabs. The trials and tribulations of taxi driving and the many bizarre experiences which befall every taxi-driver will not be found in this book, as I have had no experience of taxi driving, and there have been written at least two excellent books on the subject already.

A full list of acknowledgements will be found on page 173, but I would like in particular to thank Robert Overton and David Southwell of Mann & Overton Ltd, who entertained me and devoted a great deal of their time to answering my questions, and Jack C. Cohen who gave me the benefit of his unrivalled experiences of fifty-two years of taxi driving. I must also thank my mother and Mrs Jenny Filsell who typed out parts of the manuscript.

London 1972   G. N. GEORGANO

CHAPTER ONE

HACKNEY COACH
TO HANSOM CAB

There is no exact record of the first occasion when a Londoner called on a vehicle not his own to carry him from one place to another, but it was probably not before the beginning of the seventeenth century. Even privately-owned coaches were a rarity in the sixteenth century, largely because the streets were so uneven and full of pits and trenches of mud that wheeled vehicles had great difficulty in moving along them, and were invariably slower than a man on foot. Rapid movement in the city depended on a knowledge of short cuts down alleyways too narrow for any coach or wagon. One reason for the neglect of the roads was the much more comfortable and convenient means of transport afforded by the river Thames. Many wealthy Londoners had their own barges while the less fortunate could always share the hire of a wherry with other passengers, or take a small rowing-boat which was in the nature of a 'river taxi'. The first protest against hired coaches came from John Taylor, the poet and champion of the London watermen, who said of the coaches '... they have undone the poor trade whereof I am a member', and on another occasion,

> '... against the ground, we stand and knock our heels
> While all our profit runs away on wheels'.
> —*An Arrant Thief, 1623*

The coaches of which Taylor complained were known as hackney coaches, from the French word *hacquenée* used for a strong horse hired out for journeys and later harnessed to a plain vehicle known as a *coche à hacquenée*. In London, the first hackney coaches were to be found in the yards of the more important inns, just as today taxis are nearly always to be found outside the larger hotels. The first hackney coaches to stand for hire in the street were those owned by Captain Baily, a retired sea-captain who had served under Sir Walter Raleigh on his South American expeditions. They were relatively small vehicles, seating not more than two passengers and drawn by two horses on one of which sat the driver. Baily's coaches were said to be superior to the average, while his drivers wore livery and were given strict instructions about the fares they should charge for various journeys. In a letter to the Earl of Strafford, the Rev George Garrard wrote:

> ... here is one Captain Baily, he hath been a sea captain, but now lives on the land, about this city, where he tries experiments. He hath erected, according to his ability, some four hackney coaches, put his men in livery, and appointed them to stand at the Maypole in the Strand, giving them instructions at what rates to carry men into several parts of the town, where all day they may be had. Other hackney men seeing this way, they flocked to the same place, and performed their journeys at the same rate; so that sometimes there are twenty of them together, which disperse up and down, that they and others are to be had everywhere, as watermen are to be had by the waterside. Everybody is much pleased with it; for, whereas, before, coaches could not be had but at greater rates, now a man may have one much cheaper.

The Maypole was the site of the present church of St Mary-le-Strand, and in 1968 a thanksgiving service was held in the church, preceded by a parade of taxis old and new, and attended by many taxi drivers.

The popularity of Baily's coaches attracted other hackney men and other passengers, so that congestion and the resultant damage to the already appalling roads became a serious problem. Charles I tried to popularise a new form of transport, the sedan chair, which he had seen in Spain when, as Prince of Wales, he and the Duke of Buckingham had made their fruitless journey to Madrid in 1618 to arrange a marriage with the Infanta. Buckingham was the first person to be carried through London in a sedan chair, a present from Charles, but the general opinion was that men were degraded to the level of beasts by carrying such a conveyance. This reaction may have been due to the great unpopularity of Buckingham, and also to the position in which his chair was carried—above the bearers' shoulders. After Buckingham's assassination in 1628 the sedan chair, now carried in the more 'democratic' position with the shafts at the bearers' waists, became more popular. In 1635 Charles granted a patent to Sir Saunders Duncombe for the sole right to supply sedan chairs. The hackney-coach operators protested against this (this objection by established operators to the newcomer has continued through the early motor-cab era and the two-seater of the 1920s to the minicab war which is not yet over), and the result was a royal commission for the regulation of coaches. Hackneys were forbidden to be used in London except for carrying people to and from their homes in the country, and the same commission decreed that not even a private individual could keep a coach in the city, unless he also kept four able horses fit for His Majesty's service in time of war.

Thus threatened with the ruin of their new industry, the 'distressed hackneymen' submitted a petition in June 1636 asking that a hundred of them might be allowed to form a corporation to ply without interference. They pointed out that full-time hackney drivers in London did not number much over a hundred, and that the existing congestion was being caused by the large number of coaches which were being hired out as a speculative activity by shopkeepers. The petitioners offered to pay £500 per annum for the right to ply, but the King refused. In 1638 they offered not only the same annual payment but also volunteered to keep fifty men and horses ready for military service. This offer was also refused, so the hackneymen decided to ignore the royal proclamation. Charles evidently had more important things on his mind, especially his chronic shortage of money which made him dependant on an unsympathetic Parliament, and no hackneyman was prosecuted. Indeed, in 1639, the requested licence was granted to the Corporation of Coachmen.

There was keen rivalry between the hackney coach and the sedan chair, as evidenced by a pamphlet of 1636 entitled *Coach and Sedan Pleasantly Disputing for Place and Precedence*. In this, the arguments for both are set forth in a dialogue, with the Brewer's Cart acting as moderator. Although hackneys increased greatly in number over the next fifty years, sedan chairs did not become really fashionable until the reign of Queen Anne. In 1711, licences were granted for 200 chairs, and this was increased to 300 in the following year. The fare was fixed at one shilling (5p) a mile, making the chairs more expensive than the hackney coaches which were authorised to charge 8d (3½p) per mile. One advantage of the sedan chair was that the chairmen were tough fellows, and if their loyalty was ensured by a good tip they would defend the passenger against attack by footpads. On the other hand, they might easily be in league with the footpads, and a more general failing was that they were apt to set down the box whenever the chance appeared of a foaming tankard of ale. Sedan chairs were also owned by private individuals, in provincial towns as well as in London, but the capital had such a fine reputation for their construction that people would send from as far away as Cheltenham to have their chairs made in London. As roads became wider and better surfaced the speed of coaches increased, whereas the chair was always limited to a man's walking speed. Their use declined during the latter years of the eighteenth century, although Charles Knight (*Knight's London*, 1842)

Page 17 (above) Oxford Circus in 1891, with two hansom cabs and a barrel organ in the foreground; *(below)* a hansom cab in Regent Street, c 1905

Page 18 (above) Hansom cabby jeering at motorcab driver. An incident during the taxi drivers' strike of January 1913; *(below)* growlers at Charing Cross Station in 1913

reported that there was still one chair lingering about May-fair as late as 1841. At that date there were also still several to be had in Oxford and Bath. Knight attributed the decline of the sedan chair to growing democracy: 'When everybody rode in coaches, the lords and ladies set up their chairs. Now the times are altered; we have seen a peer in an omnibus.'

It is not known how the Civil War affected the coach trade in London, but it flourished under Commonwealth rule, and by 1654 it was necessary for Parliament to limit the number of hackney coaches in London and Westminster to 300. A few months after the Restoration, in 1660, hackney coaches were forbidden to stand in the streets, being banished to inn yards where they had been before the enterprising Captain Baily had brought them out. However, this new proclamation apparently had no more success than the previous one. Samuel Pepys wrote in his Diary for 7 November 1660, 'Notwithstanding that this was the first day of the king's proclamation against hackney coaches coming into the streets to stand to be hired, yet I got one to carry me home.' When one considers the limited resources which seventeenth-century monarchs had for enforcing civil laws in the absence of any police force, it is hardly surprising that the proclamations against hackney coaches had little effect.

In 1661 Charles II appointed commissioners to improve the condition of London streets, and one of their duties was to issue hackney-coach licences, limited to 400. Regulations were strict and forbade the granting of a licence to anyone who followed another trade or occupation, or to anyone whose horses were less than fourteen hands (4ft 8in) high. Prefer-ence was to be given to former coachmen and those who had served in the armies of Charles I and Charles II. There was great competition for these licences and the regulations gave the commissioners ample opportunity for extracting bribes. Some sample fares of the period were:

One twelve-hour day: 10s   (50p)

B

One hour: 1s 6d   (7½p)
Inns of Court to Westminster: 1s   (5p)
Inns of Court to the Tower of London: 1s 6d   (7½p)
and the same rates back again, or to any place of like
distance.

After the Great Fire of 1666, London's streets were rebuilt
wider than before, and coachmen, no longer needing to
manoeuvre their horses quite so precisely, took up their position on a box on the coach instead of riding one of the horses.
The coaches became larger, many being disused family
coaches which had been sold off by the nobility and gentry.
This practice has its parallel today when a former ducal or
mayoral Rolls-Royce finds a new life as a hire car. Family
coats of arms remained on the coaches (doubtless without the
family's consent), and there was keen competition to ride in
coaches from great aristocratic houses. Hackney coaches provided a means for the socially ambitious to ape their betters,
and this motive, or perhaps just plain high spirits, brought
about an event which had far-reaching effects on the hackney
trade. In 1694 some masked women hired a coach bearing a
well-known aristocratic crest and went for a drive in Hyde
Park, where 'they behaved disgracefully and deliberately
insulted some very distinguished people who were riding in
their private coaches.' The result was that hackney coaches
were forbidden to enter Hyde Park, a rule which was not
relaxed until March 1924 when Ben Smith, the ex-taxi-driver
Labour MP, triumphantly hired a cab in which to be driven
around the Park.

A notable improvement of the 1660s was the introduction
of glass windows for hackney coaches. These had appeared
about ten years earlier on some private conveyances (the wife
of the Emperor Ferdinand III had a small glass coach as early
as 1631), but were a mixed blessing as they frequently broke
through jolting on bad surfaces, and were expensive to replace. Samuel Pepys had to pay 40s (£2.00) for a single pane
in 1668.

A hackney coach of about 1680

The limit of 400 hackney licences was raised to 700 in 1694, by which time the demand for a licence was so great that, although the standard charge was £5, they changed hands for up to £100. The licence fee was raised to £50 by the same law of 1694, but the licence was then valid for twenty-one years. But despite these restrictions there were far more than the permitted numbers of hackney coaches plying for hire in London, especially at night. This was because those hackney men who could not obtain a licence, or were simply not willing to pay the price, moved to any small town within twenty miles of London, and entered the city by plying as stage coaches. Once on the London streets, they drove about in search of fares in open competition with the licensed coaches. The parallel with the London minicabs of the 1960s is very close, and one can be sure that the reaction of the licensed hackneymen was at least as violent as that of their twentieth-century counterparts, and probably much more so. Even if these 'stage coaches' did not ply in the city, they were a menace to the licensed coachman, who was compelled to carry a fare up to ten miles from London if required. Any return fare which he might hope to pick up would be just as likely to be snapped up by the short-stage coach.

Apart from licence evasion, there were numerous complaints against the hackneymen, who were almost as rough
and turbulent a crowd as the chairman had been. They
frequently stood in front of shops, and as there were no pavements at that time they prevented the customers from entering. When the tradesmen remonstrated with the coachmen,
they were often set upon and severely beaten. Disputes over
fares were frequent and a French visitor, Monsieur Misson,
writing in 1697 *(Memoirs and Observations of a Journey in
England)* recorded that if a gentleman offered to fight the
coachman to decide a quarrel, the latter would consent with
all his heart. Sometimes this consent would better have been
withheld; Misson says, 'I once saw the late Duke of Grafton
at fisticuffs in the open street, the widest part of the Strand,
with such a fellow whom he lammed most horribly'.

Violence was not confined to coachmen and passengers.
Thieves had adopted the practice of cutting open the backs
of hackney coaches and stealing the wigs of both male and
female passengers.

There was no great change in the position of the hackney
coach during the eighteenth century, although their numbers
continued to grow so that there were 1,000 licences by 1768,
and 1,100 in 1805. Nevertheless, there was still a shortage of
transport after the theatre, a problem by no means confined
to the twentieth century. In the 1780s, the factor Tate
Wilkinson had this experience:

> I determined to post away for the Drury Lane theatre, thinking
> I might luckily get a coach on that spot, but the getting there,
> though so short a distance, cost me many a sigh and sob, though
> I cannot say tear, but was near paying that tribute to my sorrows
> from the accumulated distresses I felt. Indeed my situation must
> be allowed disagreeable, no great coat, but wind, rain, and tem-
> pest; pushed on all sides by the link-boys, coachmen, chair-men,
> and crowd; hustled by the pickpockets; and dreading every
> moment to be thrown down by the slippery inter-mixture of snow
> and rain. [Eventually he reaches Drury Lane Theatre.] The
> universal outcry for 'coach' and 'chair' was inconceivable, and

at any price, 'half a guinea to the city', 'half a guinea to Grosvenor Square', etc. In the box-lobby I gave many marks of uneasiness, and expressions of sorrow and distress that I could not engage a coach for Gray's Inn Lane: the box-keepers then in waiting all knew me, and gave every consolation to their power, not only in words of comfort but the more pleasing promised assurance of relief at the first opportunity; for one or two of them whispered me to be quiet, and I should not be left unlike a gentleman without my carriage ... at length in loud words I heard, 'Mr Wilkinson's carriage is waiting!' On the first sound of such welcome and unexpected tidings I was at a loss how to act, supposing a Mr Wilkinson's real carriage was waiting, as there are many rich Wilkinsons as well as poor; but my stupor was relieved by the box-keeper advancing and bowing to me to attend me to my carriage. He readily explained the quick mode he had taken to relieve my impatience and anxiety, as many in waiting would suppose it was my own vehicle. I judged all my cares were over, but at the bottom of the steps I was saluted by my Cockney coachman as follows: 'Lookye, my master, I knows not whomsoever you may be, but the night is so bad it will be the death of me and my cattle, and I don't ax you for my fare, for I was not on any stand and you can't oblige me as how to take you, so minds I tells you that I won't take you into my coach, for as how to carry you to Gray's Inn Lane, without that you will give me eight shillings; and I won't because I won't, and so I tells you; but if you will give me that there price, why I will drive you as well as I can.'

I stopped his harangue and assured him I would on my honour give him eight shillings, which silenced his oration, and into the coach I got, and felt myself in a paradise, and with the utmost difficulty I was slowly dragged to my hotel, where I cheerfully paid the sum stipulated, with a bumper of brandy into the bargain; and the Jehu was so faithful on his part of assurance that when at the hotel there were three or four gentlemen in great distress for a coach, but contrary to that part of the town where his home was destined for the night, he would not accept any bribe whatever, but made his exit, exulting in the favour he had bestowed in bringing the *gemman* to his lodgings on so dismal a night.*

The best coaches were very luxurious, having been the finest of private coaches which might have cost £700 to £800, although the hackneymen seldom paid more than £25 to £50

* From *Sarah Siddons* by Roger Manvell (Wm. Heinemann Ltd)

for them. The beginning of the nineteenth century, however, saw a decline in the standards of the majority of coaches; popular taste began to favour the more lightly-built two-seater chariot in which the driver rode the nearside horse, and by the 1820s the one-horse cab began to appear as well. The hackneys became very seedy. Writing in 1825, a correspondent of *The London Magazine* said,

> A hackney coach—fogh! Who can be a gentleman and visit in a hackney coach? Who can indeed? To predicate nothing of stinking wet straw and broken windows, and cushions on which the last dandy has cleaned his shoes, and of the last fever it has carried to Guy's, or the last load of convicts transported to the hulks.

Despite the publication of books giving the regulation fares for every conceivable journey in London (one such book, published in 1805, gave 10,000 hackney-coach fares, as well as many for chair-men and watermen) *The London Magazine* correspondent, who signed himself 'Jehu', thought that coachmen were extortionate and suggested an early form of meter. It should, he said, be a pedometer,

> ...as effective against fraudulent space as a watch is against fraudulent time, with shillings on the dial plate where there are hours; and where there are minutes, sixpences. It would not cost £2, and would save endless altercations; it would save typographing a table of hackney coach fares; it would save a man's money and temper and go far towards saving the souls of hackney coachmen born, or to be born—and the trouble of the commissioners. Our invention is the best of all possible inventions, and therefore it will not be adopted.

The meter was adopted in the end, but not for another seventy-five years, so it is highly unlikely that 'Jehu' was alive to see it.

A vivid account of the decrepit state into which the hackney coach had by then fallen was given by Charles Dickens. Writing in *Sketches by Boz* in 1835, he says:

> There is a hackney coach stand under the very window at which we are writing; there is only one coach on it now, but it is a fair

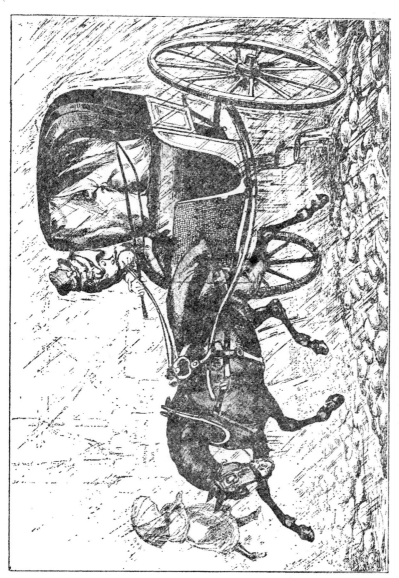

An 'outrigger' cab of 1823 with curtains drawn

specimen of the class of vehicles to which we have alluded—a great, lumbering, square concern of a dingy yellow colour (like a bilious brunette) with very small glasses, but very large frames; the panels are ornamented with a faded coat of arms, in shape something like a dissected bat, the axle tree is red and the majority of the wheels are green. The box is partly covered by an old greatcoat, with a multiplicity of capes, and some extraordinary-looking clothes; and the straw, with which the canvas cushion is stuffed, is sticking up in several places, as if in rivalry with the hay which is peering through the chinks in the boot. The horses, with drooping heads, and each with a mane and tail as scanty and straggling as those of a worn-out rocking-horse, are standing patiently on some damp straw, occasionally wincing and rattling the harness; and now and then, one of them lifts his mouth to the ear of his companion, as if he were saying, in a whisper, that he should like to assassinate the coachman.

Hackney coaches survived into the 1840s in considerable numbers, there being 400 licensed in 1841, but ten years later they had nearly all disappeared, although a few were around as late as 1858. Their replacement was the cab, the two-wheeled, single-horse *cabriolet de place* which had appeared in Paris at the beginning of the nineteenth century. The first London cabs were strictly two-seaters, which meant that the lone passenger had to sit alongside the driver. In 1823 a new form of cab appeared, built by David Davies, with seating for two passengers under a hood, but the driver was relegated to a very uncomfortable seat on the offside of the vehicle, between the wheel and the passenger compartment. A curtain could be drawn across the front of the passengers to shield them from wind and rain. Twelve of these cabriolets were put into service on 23 April 1823. A later variety was known as the 'coffin cab' from the similarity of the body of the vehicle to an up-ended coffin. At first the abbreviation 'cab' was considered very vulgar, but like many convenient words it soon became widely adopted.

Cab travelling was faster than coach travelling, but in return for speed the passenger had to put up with discomfort and sometimes danger. Cab drivers were a more adventurous

The 'coffin' cab, 1825

set of men than hackney-coach drivers, and in trying to show off their superior speed they frequently collided with lamp-posts or other vehicles. If the horse fell, the passenger was usually pitched out into the road, and this danger restricted the use of cabs to the young and the adventurous. Dandies in particular would boast of the number of times they had been thrown out of a cab. The coach drivers wondered why people trusted their necks in one of 'them crazy cabs, when they can have a 'spectable 'ackney cotche with a pair of 'orses as von't run away with no vun' (Dickens: *Sketches by Boz*). The cab drivers riposted that a hackney-coach horse was never known to run at all.

As the popularity of cabs grew, the hackney proprietors became alarmed and tried to transfer their licence plates to cabs, but for several years they were unsuccessful as the cab owners were well-connected and sometimes aristocratic men who were able to keep the trade in their own hands. They believed in the maxim that scarcity stimulates demand, and kept down the number of cabs to fifty. In 1831 the number went up to 150, and to 165 in 1832 when the monopoly was ended and hackney-coach men were allowed to transfer their licences. This was the beginning of the end for the lumbering hackney coach, and within a few weeks several hundred cabs were on the streets. A paper called *The Cab* was founded in 1832, but its title was misleading for it was a literary journal which took advantage of the prevailing fashion for cabs, rather than a trade journal. The cab trade had to wait another forty-two years before it had a journal of its own, *The Cabman*, which was published from 1874 to 1876. By 1900, a further five journals devoted partly or wholly to cabs had come and gone, with such titles as *The Cab Trade Gazette*, *Cabman & Omnibus News*, *Hackney Carriage Guardian*, and *Cabman's Weekly Messenger*.

The problem of accommodating at least two passengers and a driver in a two-wheeled vehicle exercised the minds of a number of inventors during the 1820s. William Boulnois designed a closed cab with two seats facing one another, a door at the back, and the driver perched above the bodywork, at the front. This was known as the backdoor cab, the duobus, or the minibus. Its chief drawback was that the rear exit afforded a very tempting opportunity for the passenger to slip out without paying his fare. The next design came from a

The first hansom cab, 1834

Leicestershire architect, Joseph Aloysius Hansom (1803-82) who, in 1834, patented a square-framed cab with two side-by-side seats and two doors at the front on either side of the cabby's feet. It had enormous wheels of 7ft 6in diameter, which were slightly taller than the cab itself. The wheels were carried on two short stub axles. Hansom drove this cab from Hinckley, Leicestershire, to London, a distance of 95 miles, causing much amusement and curiosity en route. It did not have a long career in its original form, but a modified version

An improved hansom cab, 1835, with smaller wheels
and windows for the passengers

with smaller wheels and windows for the passengers later
appeared in some numbers on the London streets. A company
was formed to operate these and to acquire the rights from
Hansom for £10,000. In fact, he received only £300, and that
at a later date, for the company found that there were many
defects in the cabs. One was that they were front-heavy because of the driver's forward position, and the shafts weighed
very severely on the unfortunate horse.

In 1836 John Chapman, secretary of the Safety Cabriolet
and Two-Wheel Carriage Co, made a number of improvements to the hansom cab. He moved the driver to the rear of
the vehicle, so improving the balance, and introduced the
sliding window in the roof through which the driver could
communicate with his passengers. With better balance, it now
became part of the driver's art to trim his cab and make the

load easy for his horse. With heavy passengers the shafts would come down smartly and the driver would lean backwards to take the strain off the horse's back. With one light passenger he would lean forward to bring the shafts into a horizontal position. Chapman used a cranked axle passing under the vehicle, although this was later replaced by a straight axle which necessitated cutting away the body beneath the passengers' seat. The resulting vehicle remained virtually unchanged in design until it was superseded by the motor cab early in the twentieth century. Despite Chapman's improvements, it was always known as the hansom cab. (See pictures, page 17.)

The Safety Cabriolet and Two-Wheel Carriage Co, operators of the original hansom cabs, soon purchased Chapman's patent, and during 1837 they placed fifty of the new cabs on the streets. Imitators soon appeared, and although the company successfully prosecuted several rivals they could not obtain damages as the infringers were men of no substance. After the company had spent over £2,000 on lawsuits and obtained only £500 in damages, they decided to abandon their right to the words 'Hansom's Patent Safety', which thereafter appeared on all cabs of this type. The general public might not be able to distinguish between genuine and imitation hansoms but the company's drivers certainly could, and called the rival cabs 'shofuls'. This derives from the Yiddish word for 'counterfeit', for in the 1830s, as today, the London cab trade had a large proportion of Jewish drivers.

There was a greater variety of vehicle for hire in the 1840s than at any time before or since. In addition to the hansoms there were still some aged hackney coaches, outrigger cabs and backdoor cabs, and these were joined by yet another cab, the four-wheeler, later known as the 'growler' (picture, page 18). This was similar to the single-horse, privately-owned four-wheeled carriage used by King William IV when he was Duke of Clarence, hence its alternative name of 'clarence'. It seated two passengers in the closed portion, with a third on the box beside the driver. Four-wheelers first appeared in hackney use in 1835, operated by the General Cabriolet Conveyance Co, and soon took over the hackney coaches' role as the sober and dignified end of the cab trade. Hansoms, like their predecessors the outrigger cabs, were for the young and adventurous, and they had not entirely lived down this prejudice even by 1900. H. C. Moore, writing in 1902, said: '... at the present day there are still some old ladies who will on no account enter a hansom, and shake their heads sorrowfully when they see their grand-daughters doing so'. In December 1900 *The Daily Mail* wrote that 'thirty years ago, for a couple of females from nineteen to nine-and-twenty to hail and drive alone in a hansom was a heinous social sin', although by 1900 it was apparently no longer so.

Certainly there was an undeniable thrill about riding in a hansom cab, quite unattainable either in a growler or in a motor cab. Cecil Knowlys, a friend of the author, has this to say about a hansom ride in 1909:

> Soon we were bowling down the Strand. The turnings and twistings revealed the fascinating scene of Edwardian London by night; of women beautifully gowned, escorted by men in tall hats and evening wear, including at all times an opera cloak, but rarely a cane... The headlong view trailing afar in unbroken line down Piccadilly to Hyde Park Corner, as seen from our gently rocking hansom was of a glittering procession of candle side-lamps on traffic similarly aglow, as it streamed up towards the Circus. Our horse tripped merrily along in clip-clop, clip-clop rhythm well in line, and to the music of countless harness bells jingling away like a night-time serenade.

Once Chapman's design had been standardised there were no startling changes in hansom cabs, although a modified version, known as Harvey's Tribus, appeared on the streets in 1844. It carried three passengers and the entrance was at the rear. The driver's seat was offset so that he could open and close the door, and the tribus had windows at the front as well as at the sides and rear. It would seem to have been an

Rear view of the 'Tribus' of 1844

improvement on the hansom, with more accommodation and greater weather protection, but not many were operated. Perhaps the vehicle's weight was against it.

A much appreciated improvement was the introduction, in about 1880, of solid rubber tyres on the cabs owned by the Earl of Shrewsbury and Talbot. These cabs were among the smartest in London, and carried the letters 'S.T.' surmounted by a coronet above the side windows. As the tyres rendered these cabs so silent, small bells were placed on the horses to warn pedestrians of their approach. Like most innovators, Lord Shrewsbury was not at all popular with his rivals who had to go over to rubber tyres themselves, at considerable expense. Some variations on the hansom included the court cab and the Parlour-hansom. The former was a four-wheeler but with the driver in the hansom position at the back, while Joseph Parlour's hansom of 1887 seated four passengers facing each other, and had two small rear doors one at each side of the driver's seat. It is not certain whether more than one of these ran, but there were a number of court cabs, introduced in the late 1880s, still on the road in 1902.

London's cab population increased greatly after the introduction of the hansom and the growler. In 1855 there were 2,706 licensed cabs and in 1860, 4,300. By December 1903 the total was 11,404, of which 7,499 were hansoms and 3,905 were four-wheelers. This was the greatest number ever licensed in London, for the coming of the motor cab saw a drop in numbers. Undoubtedly there were too many cabs, especially hansoms, at the turn of the century and many remained empty for much of the day. The large number of hansoms crawling in search of a fare added to traffic congestion, and in 1899 the police forbade empty cabs to proceed along the Strand or Piccadilly, compelling them to remain on their ranks until hired.

Despite the charm of the 'gondola of London', as Disraeli called the hansom, it was the hansom which disappeared first

Page 35 (above) Rational motor cabs in the Strand, 1906; *(below)* hansom cab and Renault motor cab, seen from above. Note hatch in roof of hansom for communication between cabbie and passenger

Page 36 (above) A motorcab rank beside a cabmen's shelter at Knightsbridge in 1907. The leading cab with solid tyres is a Sorex; *(below)* Renaults on a cab rank in Trafalgar Square, c 1910

The 'Parlour' hansom of 1887

when the end came for the horse-drawn cab. Their numbers
were falling compared with the four-wheeler by 1914, and
during the 1920s they were almost completely superseded by
the motor cab. In 1927 there were only twelve hansoms
licensed in London, compared with over a hundred growlers.
The latter were favoured by old ladies up from the country,
who distrusted motors but needed a roomy vehicle to carry
their luggage. The few surviving hansoms generally came out
only at night, lingering around Jermyn Street and St James's
where they might pick up a sentimentalist or a young couple
in search of an amusing novelty. The very last horse-cab

c

driver turned in his licence in 1947.

A relic of the horse-cab era which has survived the cabs themselves is the cabmen's shelter. The first of these was erected in Acacia Road, St John's Wood, at the expense of Sir George Armstrong, proprietor of *The Globe* newspaper, in order to give cabmen a meeting place other than the public-house. Since early Victorian days cabmen had had a reputation for drinking (Mayhew, in *London Labour and the London Poor: 1851*, described them as being 'of mostly intemperate habits') and one of the strictest rules of the shelters was that they should be teetotal. The Cabmen's Shelter Fund attracted support from the highest in the land, the subscription list being headed by the Prince of Wales. The Duke of Westminster provided another shelter in Maida Vale and Sir Squire Bancroft, the actor-manager of Her Majesty's Theatre, Haymarket, paid for a shelter outside his theatre which is still standing, although it has since been moved to Leicester Square.

In all, sixty-four shelters were erected in Central London, and one, in particular, attracted many aristocratic revellers in pre-night-club days when there was virtually nowhere to eat or drink in London after midnight. This was the cabmen's shelter in Piccadilly, near the Ritz Hotel, known to cabbies as the 'High Ground' and to Society as the Junior Turf Club. From Edwardian days until the mid-1920s this shelter was regularly patronised by such personalities as Lord Derby, Grand Duke Michael of Russia, Jimmy White the financier, John Sargent the portrait painter ,as well as countless Guards officers and their girl friends. In the 1920s they paid 2s 6d (12½p) for haddock, steak or chops, 1s (5p) more than the cabbies paid. Despite the teetotal rules, it was by no means unknown for champagne to be smuggled in by the revellers. Like many other shelters, the Junior Turf was destroyed by bombing during the second world war; none was replaced and many have been swept aside since the war by the introduction of one-way streets, or simply because there is not the money to keep them in good repair. At the time of writing there are no more than twelve still in use in London.

CHAPTER TWO

''UMMING BIRDS AND MORTAR CARTS'

The first suggestion of a mechanically-propelled cab in London came in 1711 and, although clearly a flight of imagination, it is worth mentioning. *The Daily Courant* of 13 January 1711 announced that 'at the Seven Stars under the Piazzas in Covent Garden is to be seen a chariot in the which a man may travel without horses, the like never made nor seen before in England; it will go for five or six miles an hour, and measure the miles as it goes.' It was 'performed by Christopher Holtumn, the first Author of an Alarum for a Pocket Watch', and it was said that a gentleman of quality had ordered one of his chariots. And this was sixty years before the first properly attested self-propelled vehicle, Nicolas Cugnot's steam gun tractor, appeared in Paris!

From 1820 to 1840 there was almost a mania for building steam buses in England, and though a few of these ran in London, no one seems to have suggested a steam cab. In fact, according to the eminent motoring historian, Michael Sedgwick, the only steam vehicles to have been used in taxi service anywhere in the world were some second-hand Stanley cars used in New Zealand during the 1920s. Electric cabs, on the other hand, have been used in many countries, and the first mechanically propelled cabs in London were driven by electricity. They were placed on the streets by the London

Electrical Cab Co Ltd, which was formed at the end of 1896. The share capital was £150,000, and the directors were an interesting cross-section of transport interests at the time. They were H. R. Paterson, a director of Carter, Paterson & Co Ltd, the well-known goods carriers, the Hon Reginald Brougham, a descendant of the Lord Brougham who gave his name to a version of the four-wheeler in 1840, H. H. Mulliner of the coachbuilding firm of that name, the Hon Evelyn Ellis, pioneer motorist and director of the Great Horseless Carriage Co, and J. H. Mace, director of the Daimler Motor Co Ltd. The general manager of the company was an electrical engineer, Walter C. Bersey, who gave his name to the cabs. These were to be built under contract by the Great Horseless Carriage Co and fitted with Mulliner bodies.

The Bersey electric cab of 1897, which had a range of 30 miles and a maximum speed of 9mph

They had 3½hp Lundell-type electric motors giving a speed of 9 mph and a range between battery-charging of thirty miles. A feature new to the cab trade was electric lighting inside and out, but this was not an attraction to everyone. H. C. Moore says, 'They were, perhaps, a little too brilliantly illuminated for the comfort of people of a bashful disposition, who were worried by the thought that as they rode along they were as conspicuous as if they were on the stage with the limelight turned on them'. The possibility that the interior lighting could be switched off, as in a modern cab, either did not occur to Mr Moore, or was not, in fact, available on the Bersey cabs.

The premises of the London Electrical Cab Co were in Juxon Street, Lambeth, and it was from here that the first twelve cabs began operating on 19 August 1897. By the end of the year there were twenty-five in use, and a further fifty were added to the fleet during 1898. Not all of them plied for hire on the streets and ranks, for some were reserved for private hire work at a charge of 25s (£1.25) a day, including the driver. The company exhibited the enthusiasm for motors and contempt for the horse customarily shown by all advocates of the new form of transport. On a wall in the Juxon Street office was a framed poem which read:

> 'I see the harness flung away,
> I hear the motor's roll,
> Another age dawns clear as day
> On my prophetic soul.'

The standard of poetry as well as the sentiments expressed were typical of the time. The company did not find it difficult to get drivers, although those cabbies who did not turn to electric cabs were at the very least sceptical, and often abusive. As one of them is reputed to have said: 'These blooming moters ain't sportsmanlike. What self-respecting gent would squat in a keb with an explosive machine under his seat?' This regardless of the fact that electric motors are

"HI! WHIP BEHIND!" "YAH! 'E AIN'T GOT NONE!"

not explosive. Cabbies were in the habit of referring to all motor vehicles as 'mortar carts', and the name quickly coined for the electric cab was 'humming bird' because of their sound and their yellow-and-black livery. A *Daily Telegraph* correspondent reported that small boys hooted when they went by, and horse cabbies shouted 'where's yer whip?', 'Where's yer nosebag?' A *Punch* cartoon showed an urchin riding on the back of a cab, and a bystander calling out the traditional 'Whip behind' to the cabbie. The urchin replies, 'Yah! 'E ain't got none!'

Taking unauthorised rides in this way was very popular with small boys, but it led to Britain's first motoring fatality on the public highway, one of two unhappy 'firsts' to the account of the electric cab. On 23 September 1897 nine-year-old Stephen Kempton was riding on the rear springs of an electric cab in Stockmar Road, Hackney, when his coat became caught in the driving chain. He was crushed between the wheel and the body of the vehicle. The other electric cab 'first' took place on 10 September 1897 when George Smith, a 25-year-old driver, was charged with drunken driving in Bond Street. He was fined £1. *The Autocar* commented sternly, 'This is an offence that should be very stringently dealt with, as an autocar in the hands of a drunken man is distinctly worse than a horse-drawn vehicle.'

Oddly enough, a drunken driver is also concerned with the first appearance of a motor cab in fiction—a Bersey electric, a type which had by then disappeared from London's streets. *The Penny Pictorial Magazine* for 29 September 1900 carried a short story entitled 'A Motor Cab Mystery', in which the body of a murdered man is found in a motor cab which is being steered 'by a very unsteady hand, running from side to side of the road in a most alarming manner.' Suspicion falls on the driver, but he is eventually cleared. His drunkenness, however, results in a fine and the cancellation of his licence.

The electric cabs were welcomed by the great Cab Drivers' Union of London, with about 10,000 members, but were opposed by the London Cab Trades Council, a proprietors' organisation. They feared that if the new cabs became really popular, they would be forced to buy large numbers of them at great expense, just as they had been obliged to emulate the rubber-tyred hansoms of Lord Shrewsbury. They also felt that the old cabbie would not become an electric-cab driver, and that the work would call for a totally different class of man, more familiar with machinery and consequently likely to demand higher wages. Ostlers and yardmen too, it was feared, would lose their jobs. The press gave favourable reports to the new cabs at first; the *Daily Telegraph* said they were 'quick, comfortable and silent', while the *Daily News* remarked, 'this electrical Pegasus is very pleasant, quiet and smooth'. The drivers were said to be among the smartest of London cabbies, and it was prophesied that the most intelligent drivers would soon leave the old type of cab for the new. One of these was Mickey More, known as the 'Demon Driver'. He had driven a hansom for sixteen years, but was now a keen convert to electricity; 'The horse is constructed on horrible principles,' he said, 'it moves in unstable equilibrium, its feet tread in line as it trots, and if one foot stumbles the other three fall over it; it is weak in the head, short-lived and constantly coming to grief.' Other enthusiasts for the Bersey cabs included the music-hall stars George Chirgwin (the 'White-Eyed Kaffir') and Minnie Palmer, who later bought a petrol-engined Daimler car for her own use.

Altogether, the future for the electric cab looked very encouraging at the beginning of 1898, but a number of defects bgan to show up after six months' constant use. Tyre wear was much heavier than had been expected, although this is hardly surprising since the same tyres were used for a 40-cwt cab as for an 8-cwt hansom. Despite the initial praise

in the press for the cabs' smoothness, they soon began to vib-
rate, especially when starting, the accumulator box slid about
and knocked against the floor of the cab, and the shoe-brake
acting on the rear tyres was also criticised. The public, which
had shown such enthusiasm for the electrics when they were
a novelty, soon returned to the familiar hansom and growler.
H. C. Moore said

'. . . while you meet hundreds of people who have had one ride
in an electric cab, you come across very few who have had two.
It is not because their experience was unpleasant that they have
not had a second one, but because it was not so enjoyable as a
ride in a horse-drawn cab. Apparently the hansom cab has every
prospect of retaining its popularity for another sixty years. (1902).

This prophecy was to prove sadly wide of the mark, but
at least the hansoms outlived the electrics.

Because of the limited range of the electric cabs, their
drivers were said to be unwilling to undertake long journeys,
although this was no doubt also because they were uncertain
of finding a return fare. A passenger once engaged an electric
cab to take him from Oxford Circus to Hampstead, but after
proceeding a short distance it stopped. 'The electric power's
gone,' said the driver. After the passenger had alighted and
paid his fare, he saw the cab proceeding merrily back to
Oxford Street, its electric power miraculously restored.

In April 1898 a new type of Bersey cab appeared, built by
the Gloucester Railway Waggon Co. It had a larger accumulator giving a speed of 12 mph, and the body was mounted
on a set of springs completely separate from the motor and
accumulator, thus eliminating vibration. A few Berseys were
running in Paris at this time, and at least one French-built
Kriéger electric cab was being used in London. *The Autocar*
thought it generally cruder than the Bersey, although they
praised its band brakes compared with the shoe brake of the
English cab.

The London Electrical Cab Co's third annual general
meeting in December 1898 included a very apologetic report

from the chairman, H. H. Mulliner, excusing the company's losses (£6,207 for the first twenty months of trading) and the shortcomings of the cabs, and promising that they would overcome their troubles. Electricity for re-charging the cab batteries was proving so expensive that the company had now set up their own generating plant. Other heavy expenses were maintenance of the accumulators and, especially, the replacement of tyres. Although continuing to keep cabs on the streets for general hire, the company intended to develop the private-hire trade, leasing cabs by the day, week or month. It was claimed that this would reduce wear and tear, private-hire work being less strenuous than plying on the streets and ranks, and that it would also avoid the need for Scotland Yard licences. Some customers, including Prince Henry of Orleans, hired electric cabs for long periods.

In December 1898 there were a total of seventy-one cabs in service, although the original plans had called for 320 within the first twelve months. They had run a total of over 200,000 miles, each cab averaging fifty miles a day. The drivers had originally paid 6s (30p) a day to hire cabs from the company, but this proved uneconomic and the rate was increased to the odd amount of 12s $2\frac{1}{4}$d (66p) a day, or about the same rate as was paid for a hansom cab. This may have been one reason why the rush of drivers which had so gratified the company at the beginning dried up after a year, although another seems to have been that breakdowns, to which the cabs were increasingly subject, caused serious financial loss to the drivers. The company was not prepared to insure them against such breakdowns, and could always say that they were caused by incompetent driving.

During 1899 some sections of the press turned against the cabs, this being part of the general distrust of the motor vehicle which was less evident when cars were extreme rarities but which built up as they became more familiar. A typical report, describing an alleged accident, said 'Hardly had this cab retired worsted from its cowardly assault on an unoffending bus when it, in its turn, was attacked from behind by its companion!' On investigation, *The Autocar* found this incident was a fabrication.

In August 1899 the debenture holders of the London Electrical Cab Co sold all the plant and cabs in order to protect their rights. Not a great deal of money was realised, as all the equipment was specialised and of little use to anyone else. Apparently no one was prepared to take over the company as a going concern, although a few electric cabs were operated for a further nine months by small proprietors. The debenture holders did not realise all their money, and the ordinary shareholders got nothing. By June 1900 there were no electric cabs running in London, or anywhere in the British Isles, although New York by that time had over two hundred, and some electric buses were in use in Berlin.

There is only one known survivor of the Bersey cabs, now on show at the National Motor Museum, Beaulieu, Hampshire.

CHAPTER THREE

THE ARRIVAL OF THE
MOTOR CAB

After the disappearance of the electric cab early in 1900, the growlers and hansoms resumed their monopoly of the London cab trade for a further four years. During this period the motorcar increased dramatically in popularity, numbers in use in Great Britain rising from about 2,000 in 1900 to 8,465 in 1904, but no mechanically-propelled cabs appeared in London. In August 1903 it was announced that fifty cabs

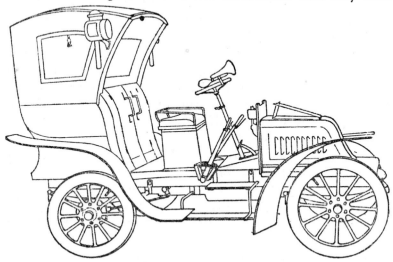

London's first petrol-engined cab, 1903

would be put into service by the Express Motor Service Co of Walbrook, London EC, but by the end of the year only one prototype was actually running. This had a 12hp two-cylinder Aster engine in a Prunel chassis, both French-built, with a hansom-style body built by Henry Whitlock & Co of Holland Gate, London. The driver sat in front of the passengers with a drop seat beside him for an extra passenger. An advanced feature for that date was an enclosed boot or trunk, for luggage at the rear of the cab, but on the whole this first motor hansom looked like the hybrid that it was. The engineer Henry Sturmey, writing in 1907, said 'I do not think a more ridiculous abortion ever made its appearance on the public roads in the guise of a vehicle'. Two more experimental Prunel motor hansoms were running in the early months of 1904, and in May of that year the Metropolitan Police Office at Scotland Yard, responsible for the licensing of London's cabs, gave approval for the first petrol-engined vehicle to ply for hire. At the end of 1904 there were still only three motor cabs in service in London.

During 1905, however, several companies were formed to operate motor cabs, and there were nineteen vehicles in service by December of that year. The most interesting of these were the Vauxhalls owned by the Metropolitan Motor Cab & Carriage Co, and the Rationals of the London Motor Cab Co. The former were true motor hansoms, with the driver perched in the traditional position, confronted not by reins but by a steering wheel on a vertical column. The steering linkage must have been distinctly complicated. The chassis was the standard 7/9hp three-cylinder Vauxhall with a three-speed gearbox and chain drive. It, and the later Brixia-Züsts from Italy, were the only taxi-cabs with three-cylinder engines to run in London. Five were operated by the Metropolitan Motor Cab Co from premises in Sussex Place, South Kensington, formerly occupied by the Locomobile Co of Great Britain. They were popular with the

The Vauxhall motor hansom cab of 1905

drivers, but passengers were less enthusiastic. Apparently the
experience of having neither driver nor horse ahead of them
was unnerving; *The Commercial Motor* noted 'even to hard-
ened motorists, the apparent rushing straight into danger
without being able to see that the driver is doing anything
to avert it must be at times disconcerting'. At least one Vauxhall was built with the driver in front sitting over the engine,
but by March 1906 they had all been withdrawn, and the
Metropolitan Motor Cab Co had turned to the French-built
Herald for its fleet.

The Rational was the product of a small company at Letch-
worth, Hertfordshire, the Heatly-Gresham Engineering Co.
It was powered by a two-cylinder horizontal 10-12hp engine,
with a two-speed epicyclic gearchange, as on the Model 'T'
Ford. An unusual feature, shared by Rational private cars,

was the use of solid rubber tyres—all other petrol-engined cabs ran on pneumatics, as did almost all private cars by this date. The Rationals themselves went over to pneumatics in 1906, after a year's service. Their top speed was 18mph, and in 1906 a Rational cab went from London to Brighton, a distance of 53 miles, in exactly three hours, which means that it must have been close to its maximum speed for the entire journey. Bodies for Rational cabs were made by Saunders of Hitchin, Wilson of Royston and Maythorn of Biggleswade. They gave full protection from the weather, and had proper doors instead of the hansom's dashboard. The London Motor Cab Co ran thirteen Rationals, beginning in the summer of 1905 and keeping them until October 1909, when they replaced them by four-cylinder Brouhots. (Picture, p 35.)

During 1906 more makes of cab were put on the road, notably the Heralds of the Metropolitan Motor Cab Co, whose fleet of fifteen was at one time the largest in London, the Simplexes of the Motor Hansom Co, and the Sorexes and Fords of the Automobile Cab Co. The Herald and the Simplex both followed the hansom pattern, the latter with the driver over the engine, while on the former he sat behind a conventional bonnet; the Sorex and Ford cabs were two-passenger landaulets indistinguishable from private cars of similar style. *The Commercial Motor* thought this a drawback, 'many fares are unfamiliar with the types of hackney motor carriages and, under the impression that they are private cars, do not hail them'. The Fords had 20hp four-cylinder engines, being based on the Model 'B' chassis. Like the later Model 'T', they had epicyclic gears. The operators announced that they were ordering two hundred, but far fewer, probably less than twenty, actually went into service. Considering its pre-eminence in the motor trade generally, the Ford Motor Co has played a negligible part in the London cab trade. Apart from an extremely brief venture with a V-8 taxi in 1936, Ford's only connection with London taxis has

Page 53
A W. & G. Napier motor cab in Piccadilly Circus in 1910

Page 54 (above) A W. & G. Panhard cab of 1910; (below) a
Renault two-cylinder-engined cab, c 1913

been to provide engines for some Beardmore and Winchester cabs of the 1950s and components for the experimental new Metrocab.

Once the motor cab showed signs of becoming established, the Metropolitan Police Office at Scotland Yard drew up a set of regulations for design and construction, as they had previously done for horse cabs. (See Appendix 2.) The insistence on a maximum turning circle of 25ft was the designer's chief bugbear, and many vehicles failed the test the first, and even the second time they were submitted. Apart from the tight turning circle, there was little difference between a cab and a small town car, so that there was no need to make a special chassis. This is why a large number of manufacturers submitted vehicles for the expected motor-cab boom, although relatively few makes were used in any numbers. Not until after World War I did private-car design progress beyond the Scotland Yard limits on matters such as interior height and ground clearance. When this happened the London taxicab had to be a specially designed vehicle, more expensive because made in smaller numbers than the mass-produced private car, and consequently the number of manufacturers wishing to cater for the taxicab trade dropped sharply.

Between 1905 and 1914 at least forty-five British and foreign car makers had cab designs licensed by Scotland Yard, but between 1920 and 1930 only twelve makes were licensed, and between 1930 and 1940 only four. The best-known makes of the pre-1914 era were the French Renault, Panhard and Unic, the Italian Fiat, and the British Napier, Wolseley, and Belsize. Other firms who catered for the taxi trade in this period included Adams-Hewitt, Argyll, Austin, Ballot, Brouhot, B.S.A. Calthorpe, Charron, Darracq, Delahaye, Dixi, D.P., Electromobile, Gladiator, Gobron-Brillié, Hillman, Leader, Lotis, Marples, Oppermann, Pullcar, Rover, Star, Straker-Squire, Thames, Vinot, West-Aster and Züst. Up

D

to 1908 they mostly had two-cylinder engines, but thereafter
the four-cylinder power unit became more widely used,
although two-cylinder Renaults were supplied in large numbers up to 1914, and some of these were still in use in 1930.
(Picture, p 54.)

The earliest motor cabs were not strictly taxis as they did
not carry a taximeter, but these were generally adopted from
1907 onwards. The history of the taximeter, or taxameter as
it was often spelt in early days, goes back much further than
the motor era. 'Jehu' in *The London Magazine* of 1825 had
called for such a device, and a meter which simply registered
distance covered was tried on a hackney cab in 1847. Called
'The Patent Mile-Index', it consisted of a dial inside the body
of the cab, visible to the passenger, showing the distance
covered. The equivalent of an hour hand measured the miles,
and the minute hand the fractions of a mile. There was another dial on the exterior of the cab which both the driver
and passenger could consult at the beginning and end of the
journey. The clock was connected to the rear axle by a
specially calibrated gear train, which was fully enclosed to
prevent its being tampered with. Neither this nor the Kilo-
metric Register of 1858 was adopted, largely because the
independent cabmen refused to allow their incomes to be
regulated in this mechanical manner. In 1891 W. G. Bruhn
of Hamburg began manufacture of a modern-type meter
which was soon adopted on cabs in Berlin, Paris, Vienna,
and Stockholm. As might be expected, it did not meet with
universal approval, and at Frankfurt-am-Main Bruhn was
thrown into the river by angry cabbies.

The taximeter was introduced to England in 1898 by the
Taxameter Syndicate Ltd, who fitted a small number of
growlers and hansoms with the device, initially in Liverpool,
Manchester, Leeds and Bradford. The first London cabs to
be so equipped were six hansoms stationed at the Hotel
Cecil in the Strand (now the site of Shell-Mex House) which

The Patent Mile-Index, one of the earliest taximeters,
installed in a hackney cab in 1847

went into service on 16 March 1899. The meter registered
distance and fare and also extras for luggage and waiting
time, and, for the cabby's information, the number of journeys made, the number of miles travelled, and the total earn-

ings of the day. Thus it was very similar to the present-day meter, although it did not calculate the fare on the basis of distance or time, as modern meters do. It did, however, carry a metal flag to indicate whether the cab was engaged or not. The flag was used in modified form on taxis until 1959, when it was replaced (on the Austin FX4) by an illuminated sign on the meter.

The introduction of the meter led to a new system of cab operation, for whereas previously the cabby had hired vehicle and horse from the owner for a fixed rate per day (about 12s [60p] in the 1890s), with meters they were to be paid an average of £2 2s (£2.10p) per week in addition to a percentage of the earnings shown on the meter. This must have appealed to a good many cabbies for it was reported that three hundred applied for the six posts offered by the Taxameter Syndicate. However the Cab Drivers' Union objected very strongly to 'the German toy' as they called the meter, and declared that any man who drove a meter cab was a blackleg. This effectively put an end to the experiment, and in less than two years the meter disappeared from London streets. Clearly a large number of cabbies were making more money by the old method, for although a fixed tariff was laid down by law, overcharging was very frequent, especially to women and others who were thought unlikely to stand up to the bullying of an irate cabby.

As there were no meters on hansom cabs in 1905, the operators of motor cabs did not see fit to install them at first. Then, in 1906, the General Motor Cab Co began experiments with a two-cylinder Renault equipped with a meter, and on 22 March 1907 the first taximeter motor cab drove out of the company's premises at the corner of Brixton Road and Camberwell New Road, premises still occupied by the company today. No sooner had the meter appeared on the motor cab than the hansom drivers wanted them too, for the fair rate implied by a meter clearly attracted the public.

Meters were made compulsory on motor cabs in July 1907, and many horse-cab owners then adopted them in order to compete, although they were never obligatory on hansoms and growlers. By the same regulations of 1907, motor-cab fares were fixed at 8d (3½p) a mile compared with 6d (2½p) a mile for horse cabs. The music-hall singer Billy Williams had a song entitled 'The Taximeter Car,' whose refrain ran 'You can do it in style for eightpence a mile.' Tips of course, were not regulated, but *Motor Traction* said in 1908, 'A tip of tuppence in the shilling will not hurt you, and a driver's smile is well worth the money.'

The motor-cab invasion really got under way in 1907, with 723 on the London streets, while by the end of 1908 the figure had reached the startling total of 2,805. The following table will give an idea of the relative position of horse and motor-cabs during the transition period. The figures are for 31 December each year.

1903	horse:	hansom	7,499	
		four-wheeler	3,905	
			11,404	
	motor:		1	total 11,405
1904	horse:	hansom	7,000	
		four-wheeler	3,924	
			10,924	
	motor:		3	total 10,927
1905	horse:	hansom	6,850	
		four-wheeler	3,910	
			10,760	
	motor:		19	total 10,779
1906	horse:	hansom	6,500	
		four-wheeler	3,824	
			10,324	
	motor:		96	total 10,420

1907	horse: hansom	5,923	
	four-wheeler	3,866	
		9,789	
	motor:	723	total 10,512
1908	horse: hansom	5,095	
	four-wheeler	3,754	
		8,849	
	motor:	2,805	total 11,654
1909	horse: hansom	3,299	
	four-wheeler	3,263	
		6,562	
	motor:	3,956	total 10,518
1910	horse: hansom	2,003	
	four-wheeler	2,721	
		4,724	
	motor:	6,397	total 11,121
1911	horse: hansom	1,054	
	four-wheeler	2,293	
		3,347	
	motor:	7,626	total 10,973
1912	horse: hansom	567	
	four-wheeler	1,818	
		2,385	
	motor:	7,969	total 10,354
1913	horse: hansom	386	
	four-wheeler	1,547	
		1,933	
	motor:	8,397	total 10,330
1914	horse: hansom	232	
	four-wheeler	1,159	
		1,391	
	motor:	7,260	total 8,651

The number of companies operating cabs mushroomed during this period; two of the largest were the previously-mentioned General Motor Cab Co (now the London General Cab Co) and the United Motor Cab Co, which operated French-built Unic cabs. This became one of the best-known makes of London taxi, and remained so until the 1930s. They were sold by Mann & Overton Ltd, motor retailers since 1899, until Unics ceased to be imported. Mann & Overton then obtained the concession for the sale of Austin cabs which they still hold today, and they estimate that they have supplied about 75 per cent of all London taxicabs since 1906. The original Unics had 10/12hp two-cylinder engines, supplemented by four-cylinder 12/14hp models in 1908. During 1907-8 the United Motor Cab Co bought 224 Unics and 250 Darracqs. The General Cab Co bought 500 Renaults during the same period, and in the autumn of 1908 the two companies, already the giants of the London cab trade, merged to form the London General Cab Co with a fleet of close on 1,000 vehicles. Other big operators at this time included the Fiat Motor Cab Co, with 400 10/14hp four-cylinder Fiats, the London United Motor Cab Co with 250 two and four-cylinder Wolseley-Siddeleys, and the London & Provincial Cab Co with 100 Wolseley Siddeleys. It will be seen that the majority of cabs were of foreign manufacture and, since all the meters were also foreign, a great cry went up from the horse-cab faction that the motor-cab trade was unpatriotic and dominated by foreign trusts. Questions were asked in Parliament, but it was shown that although some companies, such as the Fiat Motor Cab Co, had one foreign director on the board, they were otherwise wholly British. In any case, within a few years British motor cabs such as Argyll, Belsize and Napier came onto the streets in some numbers, although it was noticeable that French makes remained popular for another twenty years.

The design of motorcabs was generally conventional, with

front-mounted two or four-cylinder engines of modest size and power (seldom over 2½ litres capacity and 20bhp), three-speed gearbox and shaft drive. In *Motor Traction's* Buyers' Guide for 1909 there were thirty-six makes of taxicab available, and all had shaft drive except the Albion (chains) and the Pullcar (chains to front wheels). The latter was a highly unusual vehicle which, in its original 1906 form, had pneumatic tyres on its front driving wheels, and solids on the much larger rear wheels. The body was of the hansom type, and could indeed be a genuine hansom modified to fit onto the 'half chassis' or *avant train* carrying the power unit and drive system. The driver sat over the 10/12hp two-cylinder Fafnir engine which drove the front wheels via epicyclic gears and double-chain final drive. It was planned to put 300 Pullcars into service, but very few, if any, actually plied for hire. By 1909 the fashion for motor hansoms was dead, and later Pullcars had equal-sized wheels and a four-cylinder White and Poppe engine.

Other unconventional designs included the 1906 Adams-Hewitt with single-cylinder horizontal engine and pedal-operated gears ('Pedals to Push—That's All' was the company's slogan), and the 1907 D.P. (Dawfield, Phillips) with two-cylinder horizontal engine mounted halfway between the front and rear axles driving the latter by a single chain. The better-known cab designs, however, went in for none of these eccentricities. There were still a few electric cabs but they seemed to be more popular with private-hire firms who leased them by the day, month, or year. In 1908 the Electromobile Co built a solid-looking machine with chassis by Greenwood & Batley of Leeds and body by the Gloucester Carriage and Waggon Works. It was operated by the Electromobile Taxicab Co and was intended to replace the growler for station work where heavy luggage was involved. It was announced that 500 Electromobiles were to go into service, but not more than twenty in fact did.

In the beginning, the motor cab was much more of a threat to the hansom than to the growler, for it seated only two passengers and had limited luggage capacity. Four-seaters began to appear during 1908, most of them on four-cylinder chassis. The additional seats were rear-facing, as on all London cabs until very recently (forward-facing occasional seats were introduced on the Austin FX4 hire car in 1971). For carrying more than two passengers an extra charge of 6d ($2\frac{1}{2}$p) per passenger was levied, which also applied to growlers. A misunderstanding about this charge led to the first strike of motor-cab drivers, though it was not a very serious one. In order to ensure that the correct charge was made for an extra passenger, the London General Cab Co put notices in all their four-seater cabs telling passengers not to pay any fare except that which was recorded on the meter. The drivers took this to mean a prohibition of accepting tips, and its ambiguity may have led parsimonious passengers to think the same. After a strike of a few days' duration the offending notices were removed. Soon the four-seater cab became the standard model, and any attempt to introduce smaller cabs (see Chapters 6 and 8) have met with the strongest opposition.

The early motor cabs were often spartan vehicles whose bare and uncomfortable interiors were put to shame by the more luxurious of the hansoms. However, the Fiat and the Beeston Humber were above average from the start, and touches of luxury soon began to appear. The Darracqs, for example, had foot-warmers heated by exhaust gases, while electric light and a speaking-tube between passengers and driver were to be found on a number of cabs. The 1909 Fiat had an indicator which could be operated by the passengers, showing 'Left', 'Right', 'Faster', 'Slower', 'Home', a feature borrowed from private-car practice. Owners also allowed their imagination free rein in the external appearance of cabs, one fleet being painted orange with panel beading in broad black lines. The Ballots operated by the Quick Motor

Cab Co were all-white, while the Leader cabs were painted in an attractive shade of French grey, outlined in black.

In general, it was the smaller operators who had the smartest vehicles. One such was C. MacBean & Co of Pelham Street, South Kensington, who had eight Unic 12/14hp cabs with bodies by Christopher Dodson of Westminster. The panelling, in two shades of green, was made of compressed paper instead of wood, this being easier to replace in the event of an accident. The interiors included a mirror, ashtrays and a vase which was filled with fresh flowers each morning. Mr MacBean's crest was reproduced on the door panels and on the drivers' caps and buttons. Most of this company's work was in the private-hire field. In 1909 a Fiat taxi was fitted with Rudge-Whitworth detachable wire wheels as used on many better-class private cars. They were light in weight and of smart appearance, but their extra cost prevented them becoming popular on cabs, which continued to rely on the old-style artillery wheel.

A new operator to appear during 1909 was the Acton firm of W. & G. du Cros. They rapidly built up a fleet of over 1,000 cabs of Panhard and Napier make, identifiable by their yellow bonnets and the letters 'W. & G.' on the radiator. (Pictures, pp 53 and 54.) The latter feature has led some people to think of 'W. & G.' as a make of cab, and this belief was re-inforced by the fact that du Cros *did* make vans, lorries, buses and ambulances of their own in the 1920s. In July 1910 W. & G. drivers announced that they would not smoke when carrying a fare, except with his or her permission.

From about 1910 onwards there were many complaints in the general and trade press that London's motor-cab fleets had grown too rapidly. Drivers often had to wait on a rank for up to three hours before finding a fare, and this despite the fact that there were fewer cabs of all kinds than at the turn of the century. One firm, the National Motor Cab Co of Hammersmith, converted many of their Unic cabs to travellers' broughams or delivery vans because of the shortage of cab work. There were three main categories of taxi traveller, the well-to-do who used them regularly for shopping and theatre journeys, people crossing London from one railway terminus to another, and a small percentage of middle-class business people. The latter, however, were making increasing use of the rapidly spreading network of metropolitan and underground railways, trams and motor buses. Very few, if any, of the working class used taxis, and indeed taxis never ventured into the poorer parts of London, knowing that it would simply have been a waste of time. In 1910 *Motor Traction* said, 'It is practically impossible during the day or night to hire a taxicab in the borough of Bermondsey, the reason being probably that the locality is so poverty-stricken that no cabman will go there in search of fares'. The borough council of Bermondsey had recently voted £5 per month to its medical officer of health for cab fares, but he was so seldom able to make use of the money that the council bought him a bicycle instead.

At the other end of the social scale, taxis began to be used by the aristocracy. *Motor Traction* reported with pride in 1909, 'The motor cab—essentially till now a democratic vehicle—is becoming the carriage of all classes. Last week Princess Louise (Duchess of Argyll) and the Duke of Argyll used one of these vehicles to convey them from London to the Princess Louise Girls' Home at Kingston Hill where they were due to present the prizes'. Presumably the cab was ordered beforehand and not simply picked up from the rank by the duke and duchess. Private hire was becoming an increasingly important part of the cab owner's trade. Before the motor car came into widespread use, a Sunday jaunt into the country by taxi was a popular form of outing for the middle-class family who disdained the plebeian charabanc. Thomas Cook & Sons arranged taxi journeys for American

tourists to such places as Stoke Poges and Windsor, and sometimes visitors would charter a cab to tour for a month or
two all round England and Scotland.

Such tours would usually be arranged in advance, but
taxi drivers had a number of tales to tell of being hired off
the rank and finding themselves embarked on a journey of
several hundred miles. One driver of an Argyll was hired in
Bishopsgate in the City and asked to drive to Ipswich, and
then to Norwich, eventually finding himself on a circular
tour through Suffolk, Norfolk and Cambridgeshire during
which he covered 350 miles in two days. What his family
thought of his sudden disappearance is not recorded. As
private-car hire became more widespread this practice declined, but as late as 1929 a Morris Commercial driver was
hired by an American couple outside the Hotel Cecil and
taken to Maidenhead, followed by increasingly lengthy
journeys to Canterbury, Torquay, Malvern and Windermere.
The following year the Americans returned and made longer
journeys in the same cab, including one to John o' Groats, in
Scotland. They came to England for five consecutive years,
during which time the Morris Commercial clocked up over
20,000 miles on these journeys alone. Its regular load consisted of two passengers and eleven trunks and cases, which
it had to carry over all surfaces of road and some of the
stiffest hills in the country.

Apart from these long journeys, taxis left the streets of
London for stranger purposes, one of the most unusual being
to race at Brooklands. In July 1909 twelve Fiat cabs were
hired for the day from the Fiat Motor Cab Co and allotted
to entrants by a draw. Each cab carried two passengers and
had to be 'in London hiring trim'. The race was won by
Harvey du Cros at the very respectable speed of nearly
33mph.

As shown in the table on pp 59-60, the horsecab was in
serious decline from 1910 onwards. The growler had always

THE PASSING OF THE GROWLER.

Mr. Punch (supported by shades of two of his most famous henchmen, John Leech and Charles Keene). "GOOD-BYE, OLD FRIEND. YOU'VE BEEN VERY USEFUL TO ME, BUT YOUR DAY IS DONE."

This cartoon appeared in *Punch* twelve days after the first General Motor Cab Co's Renault started to ply for hire. Ironically, it was not the growler but the hansom which was the first victim of the motor cab been accorded precedence by hotel porters who gave one blast on a whistle to summon a four-wheeler, two for a hansom and three for a motor cab. In 1908 the motor was promoted to one blast and the poor growler relegated to three. At least one hotel, the Carlton in the Haymarket, tried to do away with whistling by erecting an illuminated sign reading 'T' for taxicab, 'H' for hansom and 'F' for four-wheeler. This was in 1910 but the idea does not seem to have been generally adopted as complaints about whistling continued, and it was forbidden during the 1914-18 war as it disturbed wounded soldiers in hospital.

In 1909 nearly 800 horses and 200 cabs were sold in a period of six months by one dealer alone. The horses fetched from £10 to £40, the cabs little more than £1 each. Some may have gone to provincial cab operators, but the great majority were broken up. The hansom cab was said to be practically extinct in Oxford Street in 1912. The doorman of a well-known store whistled in vain for twenty minutes for one, and in the end the fare was obliged to take a motor cab. In May 1912 a hansom was presented to the London Museum in Kensington Palace. The growlers lasted longer because of their luggage accommodation, and also because motor cabs were not allowed into railway stations until 1910. The reason for this was that if the railway companies had allowed these 'explosive machines' onto their premises they would have had to pay higher insurance premiums.

The 1914-18 war and consequent shortage of petrol brought no reprieve for the horse cabs, largely because there were as many cabs off the road through lack of drivers as of petrol. The 1916 *Motor Traction* census on Putney Bridge showed no horse cabs during a whole day's observation. In 1917 the census revealed one extremely decrepit growler 'possibly being dragged into town to be chopped up for firewood'. However, the Edgware Road census of December 1917 showed thirty-three horse cabs, or 3.05 per cent of the total. Presumably horse cabbies no longer ventured out as far as Putney.

At first, the war did not cause a serious dislocation of the cab trade, and the taxi driver who was summoned in May 1915 for having six passengers in his cab, two standing, was perhaps motivated more by greed than any effort to ease the cab shortage. He pleaded that the same thing happened in buses, and that on his way to the Derby he had counted eighty overloaded cabs. He was fined ten shillings. *Motor Traction's* annual Fleet Street census showed no drop in the number of cabs between 1914 and 1915, although the number of buses fell from 3,551 for the day to 2,744. However, by the end of 1915, nearly 10,000 taxi drivers from London and the provinces had joined the forces, or about one-third of the total labour force in the trade. A number of cabs were laid up, and those still in use were often engaged for the transport of wounded and convalescent soldiers, free of charge. The introduction of conscription in February 1916 reduced the number of drivers still further, although fewer taxi drivers were called up than bus drivers; the latter's fitness and age corresponded more to military requirements, said *Motor Traction*.

Because of the driver shortage, two drastic steps were suggested; that there should be some relaxation of the Scotland Yard driving test, and that women should be allowed to drive taxis. *Motor Traction* was very much against the first suggestion, claiming that the standard of driving was bad enough already, and that some companies were notorious for the indifferent capabilities of their men. Bad driving was rendered even more dangerous by the blackout. The question of women drivers had been raised in 1908, and the Public Carriage Office at Scotland Yard had stated firmly: 'Licences to act as hackney carriage drivers are not granted to females'. A certain Sheila O'Neill got round this by driving a cab in a semi-private capacity for some businessmen, and celebrated

her triumph by mounting on the bonnet of her cab a small
metal figure of a policeman with his hand perpetually up-
raised ordering her to stop. Behind this disregarded warning
she drove happily for several years. In February 1917 the
Home Secretary relaxed the prohibition against women drivers despite opposition from the Commissioner of Police and
the taxi drivers. A threatened strike was only averted because
very few women applied to take the tests, and none passed.
There were quite a number of women drivers in provincial
cities such as Cardiff, Manchester and Edinburgh, but the
task of cab-driving in London was felt to be much more
arduous. The suggestion was brought up again in September
1917, but again no women passed, and in fact no woman up
to the present time has held the green badge which is issued
to taxi drivers authorised to cover the whole of London.

Petrol rationing was introduced in Britain in July 1916.
The original allocation was one and a half gallons per day,
later increased to two gallons, for each licensed driver, as
one cab often had two drivers, one for day and one for night
work. Car owners who had laid their vehicles up because of
petrol rationing took to hiring cabs by the week for their
essential town journeys, thus further depleting the number
of cabs plying for hire on the streets. The increasing overcrowding and discomfort on the buses led to a still greater
demand for taxis, while soldiers on leave and highly-paid
munitions workers provided a new class of taxi user. This
was the era when girls selected companions for the evening
not because they were amusing or good dancers, but simply
because they were good taxi-getters; a time when taxis were
hired to wait all through a dance by scrupulous young men
to ensure a journey home, and sometimes snapped up by
unscrupulous young men who would pay what was on the
clock and a bribe besides. Eventually, the petrol shortage
became so acute that the public was asked not to use taxis
except when really necessary. But at least Londoners were

Page 71 (above) A Unic cab of 1923. Note 'white-washed' tyres; (below) a Beardmore cab of the same year

Page 72 (above) Chassis of 1925 Beardmore cab, showing the dropped frame; *(below)* four-seater Beardmore cab (left) with 1926 Berliet prototype two-seater cab

not so badly off as Berliners, whose taxi tyres were then being made of skins stuffed with feathers.

By June 1918, many more cabs were off the road, due mainly to the Home Secretary's refusal to allow any increase of fares, despite a general feeling that the public would not have minded it. The result was much bitterness among cab owners who could not make a profit because of the increased cost of petrol, and among the drivers who were charged a halfpenny per mile driving charge by the now desperate owners. Local strikes by taxi drivers were frequent during 1918, adding to the problems of a war-weary public. By the end of the war, in November 1918, London's taxi fleet was down to less than 3,000, and the days of the really large fleet owner had gone for ever.

E

CHAPTER FOUR

OWNERS, DRIVERS AND PUBLIC

Since the beginning of the hackney trade the interests of cab
owners and drivers have been in frequent conflict, with the
public often making a third party in the acrimony. This
chapter examines the main causes of dispute up to 1918 and
also considers the position of the owner-driver, a profession
which became much more widespread with the coming of the
motor cab.

The first recorded cabmen's strike took place in 1853
against a government decision that the fare of 8d (3½p) per
mile should be reduced to 6d (2½p) per mile. On the first day,
26 July, it was limited to withdrawal of cabs from the Houses
of Parliament, drivers declining 'in most unparliamentary
language' to take members home. The following day all
London cabmen were on strike, fully supported on this
occasion by their employers. There followed a classic case
of blackleg action, with the police permitting unlicensed
cabs to ply for hire. It seems that there were plenty of cabmen
willing to do this, and after four days the licensed cabmen
were sufficiently alarmed to call off their strike. One can
hardly imagine that today's Licensed Taxi Drivers' Association would react so meekly to unrestricted plying for hire
by minicabs! However the cabmen did win some concessions,
including an increase in the cab radius from three to four
miles and a reduction in cab tax from 10s (50p) a week to
1s (5p) per day. In 1867 a minimum fare of one shilling was

introduced to cover the first two miles. Thus although the rate was the same as before, a short journey became more profitable to the cabman and more expensive to the passenger. On 1 January 1870, a regulation came into force compelling cab proprietors to display a list of fares inside each cab.

Tips, or the lack of them, were a constant source of friction between cab drivers and the public. In Wilkie Collins' book *The Moonstone* (1868), Miss Drusilla Clack comments, 'I paid the cabman exactly his fare. He received it with an oath, upon which I instantly gave him a tract... he jumped up on his box and with profane exclamations of dismay, drove off furiously. I sowed the good seed in spite of him, by throwing a second tract in at the window of the cab'.

Until the introduction of meters, cabmen hired vehicle and horse from the proprietors at a fixed rate per day. Consequently the driver's first task was to cover the hiring fee, for if he failed to do this his day's labour was entirely wasted. In the early 1890s the fee was 16s (80p) or 17s (85p) a day, which meant that even with tips a driver had to cover about twenty-five miles *before* he earned a penny for himself or his family. No wonder that they sometimes charged more than the regulation fare. In May 1894 the Cab Drivers' Union asked the proprietors to reduce the daily charge by 3s (15p). This request was refused by the major proprietors, and after a midnight mass meeting at the Novelty Theatre, which was so crowded that an overflow meeting had to be held in the street, a strike was called for the following day. London was not, however, entirely bereft of cabs for a number of the smaller owners had agreed to the union's demands. Privately-owned cabs were also on the streets, carrying a notice, 'Fair-priced cab'. About 9,000 cabs were off the streets for nearly a month and the fact that this caused surprisingly little dislocation of the Londoner's life confirms the frequently made assertion that there were too many cabs on the streets—

about 12,000 at that time. An absence of cabs after the theatre was the public's most frequent complaint.

On 11 June the Home Secretary, H. H. Asquith, made an award to drivers which varied the hiring rate according to the season, the summer rate being higher as it was assumed that drivers would get more business then. The award for hansoms was as follows:

June 4 to	July 15	six weeks at 16s per day
July 16 to	July 22	one week at 15s per day
July 23 to	July 29	one week at 14s per day
July 30 to	August 5	one week at 13s per day
August 6 to	August 12	one week at 12s per day
August 13 to	August 19	one week at 11s per day
August 20 to	October 21	nine weeks at 10s per day
October 22 to	October 28	one week at 11s per day
October 29 to	January 14	eleven weeks at 12s per day
January 15 to	April 1	eleven weeks at 11s per day
April 2 to	April 15	two weeks at 12s per day
April 16 to	May 6	three weeks at 13s per day
May 7 to	May 20	two weeks at 14s per day
May 21 to	June 3	two weeks at 15s per day

*(The present decimal currency equivalent
to the shilling is 5 pence)*

The above scale is to regulate the net cash price to be paid per day by driver to owner for first-class street hansom cabs from this date. It is to be the subject of revision as from the first Monday in April 1895, if within fourteen days prior to that date notice demanding revision is given to me by, or on behalf of, either of the parties to the agreement of this day.

The rates for iron-tyred four-wheelers with two horses per day were slightly lower, but rubber tyres cost one shilling more per day. If the four-wheeler driver wanted only one horse per day the rate was considerably lower, but then he presumably got about town pretty slowly by the end of the day, and doubtless the public were adept at spotting, and keeping clear of, a tired horse. The Asquith award was dated 11 June 1894, and the men went back to work two days later.

An Act which was greatly welcomed by cabmen was the

Taxi. "WAT'S THE MATTER WIV YOU?"

Hansom. "THERE AIN'T NOTHING THE MATTER WIV ME."

Taxi. "THEN WHY DID YOU GIVE ME SUCH A NASTY LOOK?"

Hansom. "I DIDN'T GIVE IT YER; YOU 'AD IT TO START WIV."

so-called 'Bilking Act' of 1896. Previous to this, a cabman had no redress if a fare left him outside a large shop or hotel on the pretext of getting change, disappeared inside and left by another exit. The Act made such a person liable to a fine of £2 or fourteen days in prison, part of the fine to go to the cabman in compensation, although if the bilker could not be caught, as was often the case, the cabby was no better off. This method of bilking is still practised today, or would be if taxi drivers were not extremely wary of letting a fare disappear into any building with more than one exit.

With the introduction of meters on cabs in 1907 a new system of payment came into use. The driver no longer paid for the use of the cab, but was allowed 25 per cent of the regular meter reading and, in addition, all extras including, of course, tips. He had to pay for petrol used, originally at the current trade rate but, after 1911, at a fixed rate which evened out fluctuations in the current price. Motor-cab drivers had to pass four tests, substantially the same as today:

1 A medical test ('If there is evidence of past or present excesses in the absorption of alcohol, his name is immediately struck off the list!)
2 A geographical test of London by Scotland Yard, known as 'The Knowledge'.
3 A driving test conducted by Scotland Yard examiners.
4 A thorough examination of the applicant's past life and character.

Of these four tests, the Knowledge was, and is, the most exacting, and the one which sets the licensed taxi driver in an altogether different class from the private-hire or minicab man. It was divided into two parts, the first being a knowledge of the location of important buildings, and the second of routes across London. In the first part, the driver had to know the whereabouts of all railway stations, police-courts and county courts, and of six each of the principal clubs, hospitals, hotels, squares, theatres and public buildings. In recent years the list has been extended to include every cinema, theatre, hospital and museum in the Metropolitan area, and a very large number of hotels, as well as buildings such as the Mansion House, Stock Exchange, Bank of England, and the homes of the Livery Companies. Once these have been learnt the real knowledge begins, for it is of little use to know the whereabouts of buildings if the driver cannot find his way quickly from one to another. In theory, a taxi driver should be able to take a fare to any address within a six-mile radius of Charing Cross, and taxi travellers will know that it is very rare for a driver to be at a loss. One of the difficulties presented by London streets is the number which have basically similar names, such as Kensington Palace Gardens, Kensington Park Gardens, Kensington Park Road, Kensington Gardens Square, Kensington Court, Kensington Court Place, etc.

A driver's knowledge is based on about four hundred basic routes, to which additions can be made at either end. A basic route might be from Notting Hill Gate to Waterloo; if a fare hailed the cab at Shepherd's Bush and wanted to go to the Elephant and Castle, this would involve a short extension at each end of the basic route. However a driver may have to vary his route according to the time of day (Oxford Street after midnight is an ideal thoroughfare, but during rush hours it may well be quicker to take a slightly longer route which avoids it), and he also has to know about temporary diversions and one-way-street regulations.

For a novice to reach a 'pass' standard in the Knowledge took about six months in 1907, but today he is lucky if he passes in less than twelve to fifteen months, and two years is not unknown. In fact, about 75 per cent of the applicants for a hackney-carriage licence never complete the course. The time-honoured method of learning London is to arm oneself with a large street map, a piece of cotton and some pins, and work out the shortest route between various key points. Drivers then go out over the routes, checking all important buildings, roads crossing the routes and one-way streets. This used to be done on a bicycle, but now most 'butter boys', as candidates are called, use mopeds with clip-boards attached to the handlebars. Each evening drivers test each other on the routes they have been learning.

When a 'butter boy' considers that he is ready for his first knowledge test (usually after about two months on his moped) he goes to New Scotland Yard where an examiner asks a series of questions such as 'How would you take me from the Savoy Hotel to Paddington Station?' If he cannot answer, the candidate says 'No, sir', and is told to come back in a week, or a month, according to his performance. When he has reached a good standard on the whole of London, he will be tested in greater detail on areas in which he has shown weakness, then on a general knowledge of the suburbs and of through routes to airports and racecourses. Finally, a pass on the Knowledge is granted, and the 'butter boy' is ready to take the driving test. This is much more rigorous than the ordinary Ministry of Transport test, which did not exist in 1907, and must be taken on a taxi. Men who are quite accustomed to driving private cars find that cabs take some getting used to, and if an applicant fails his driving test three times he is very unlikely to be given another chance, so all his months of painstaking work on the Knowledge are wasted.

The medical test can be conducted either by the applicant's own doctor, or if any query is raised, by a police medical specialist. It is straightforward and designed to ensure satisfactory eyesight and hearing, and to eliminate anyone with epilepsy or serious heart trouble. There is no age barrier, but it is unlikely that a man over fifty would consider beginning a new career as a taxi driver; though in Edwardian times, a number of elderly horse cabbies did apply for motor-cab licences. So long as he can pass regular health tests, there is no age at which a driver is deprived of his licence. After sixty-five he must be tested every year. In 1930 there were over a hundred drivers aged seventy or more, and one of eighty-one. At the time of writing (December 1971) London's oldest working driver is 77-year-old Jack Cohen.

The character test is really an examination of any brushes with the police, but it is very strict, and even a charge of riding a bicycle without lights is taken into account. Any criminal conviction instantly debars a driver from obtaining a licence. When one considers all these hurdles that face the licensed taxi driver, none of which has to be passed by a mini-cab driver, one can more readily understand the hostility of the taxi trade towards the minicabs, as will be seen in Chapter Eight.

At first there was a great deal of friction between the Cab Drivers' Union and the new motor drivers who were expelled from the union as soon as they drove a motor cab. They formed their own Motor Cab Drivers' Protection Association in 1907 but their first meeting ended in disorder, as horse cabmen were present. In 1910 the London Cab Drivers' Union was formed to look after the interests of motor-cab drivers, who were by then in the majority, and since 1922 taxi drivers have come under the Transport and General Workers' Union (Cab Drivers' Section). Through the years there have been a number of other taximen's organisations, of which the most recent is the Licensed Taxi Drivers' Association, founded in 1967.

As early as 1909 it was realised that the older horse-cab drivers were in a very difficult position. As a result of a letter by Lord Rosebery to *The Daily Mail,* that newspaper started a fund for the relief of horse-cab drivers who had lost their jobs. *Motor Traction* considered that, for old drivers, there was no other course but to accept the charity offered. Young drivers would be welcomed by motor-cab companies, middle-aged men less so, but they could perhaps buy their own cabs on hire purchase and thus be their own masters. In response to *The Daily Mail* appeal, Friswells, a well-known firm of motor dealers, offered to train twenty-five men to drive motor cabs free of charge. An instructor said that men who had driven horse cabs would be easier to teach than those who had had no experience at all.

In February 1909 a deputation of motor-cab drivers had a meeting with the Home Secretary, the Permanent Under-Secretary and the Commissioner of Metropolitan Police also being present. The drivers complained that the police were unduly harsh on them, revoking licences on insufficient grounds and refusing licences because of offences committed when operating horse-drawn vehicles. They wanted more than three attempts at the driving test and said that the men on the rank had insufficient time for meals. The Home Secretary was substantially in agreement with the deputation, but said there was a certain amount of irritation among members of the public who had nearly been run over by cabs, or thought they had nearly been run over, the latter class being much greater than the former.

New regulations were introduced in 1910 which, among other matters, improved the meal-time situation. So long as there were other cabs on the standing, a driver could place his cab on a reserve rank and absent himself for half-and-hour for a meal. Before leaving, he had to obtain from the nearest policeman a card which he hung on his meter reading,

> By virtue of the powers vested in me for preserving order at standings, permission has been given to the Driver of this cab to be absent for THIRTY MINUTES for meal time. During such period therefore the cab is
>
> NOT FOR HIRE
>
> *The Commissioner of Police*
> *for the Metropolis.*

At first, the motor-cab drivers were thought to have better

manners than their predecessors and their tips were proportionately higher. But as the novelty of motors wore off tips dropped, to the dismay of drivers who then asked for higher wages (which meant higher fares) or a rebate on the petrol tax. In 1911 the Home Secretary set up a departmental committee on fares to which both owners and drivers made reports. They are worth summarising as they illustrate the main problems of the pre-1914 cab trade, and are not entirely irrelevant today. In asking for an increase in tariff from 8d to 10d for the first mile, the owners argued their case as follows:

(i) Gross takings had fallen off greatly over the previous twelve months, and after paying the drivers 25 per cent commission there was insufficient money left to defray running expenses, especially tyres.

(ii) They claimed that 75 per cent of extras should go to them instead of being taken by drivers, as was almost always the case.

(iii) They did not receive the full percentage of earnings on long-distance runs where a bargain was made between driver and passenger.

(iv) Tampering with meters was a frequent occurrence, and increasing.

(v) Some lazy drivers neglected to work a cab in its proper manner, being apparently satisfied with a small daily earning.

The drivers' main complaints were:

(i) Their promised net earnings of 7s (35p) per day had not been maintained. They wanted this figure, at least, to be guaranteed, and some asked for a minimum of 10s (50p) per day.

(ii) Taxi-driving placed a strain on the health and carried a high rate of life insurance.

(iii) They suffered loss through breakdowns, false calls, bilking and tips at garages. (*Motor Traction* rejected the

last complaint, saying that tips were an inducement to
others to do work which the drivers ought to do for
themselves.)
(iv) They had to take out two licences per year, one from
the London County Council and one from the police,
at 5s each.
The Committee's main recommendations were as follows:
 (i) There should be no increase in the tariff.
 (ii) All extras should belong to the driver.
(iii) The driver's share of the takings should be 20 per cent
of the first one pound, and 25 per cent thereafter.
(iv) Owners should supply drivers with petrol at a fixed rate
of 8d per gallon, independent of market variations so
long as these did not exceed 20 per cent.
 (v) There should be no limit to the number of cabs in service.
(vi) One of the two 5s licences should be abolished.
It should be realised that these were recommendations and
had no legal force behind them. Despite the clause about
extras, in November 1911 the London Motor Cab Proprietors
Association announced that they intended to appoint observ-
ers to see that 75 per cent of extras were handed over to the
owners. A driver said that the owners would never collect the
extras unless a policeman were carried on the running-board
of each cab. The London Cab Drivers' Union then called a
meeting, which decided on strike action. A total of 7,000 cabs
were taken off the streets, but within less than a week they
were back, having won the right to keep extras, in return
paying sixpence a day 'hiring fee' to the owners. About 1,500
driver-owned cabs remained on the streets and were issued
with permits to ply by the LCDU in the form of a pennant.
It was claimed that these infringed the bye-laws forbidding
advertisements on cabs, and the police ordered their withdrawal. The strike ended before the matter could become an
issue, and in March 1912 a court of arbitration confirmed that

all extras belonged to the drivers, who should also receive 25 per cent of the meter reading. It also confirmed the sale of petrol at the fixed price of 8d a gallon for one year. *Motor Traction* complained that this decision was on the side of the drivers, and would encourage overloading. To support this, they gave the following examples:

> Charing Cross to Piccadilly, four men in one cab; 8d for two passengers; 6d each for two extra passengers; 2d each for two suitcases. Total: 2s, of which the owner gets 8d less 25 per cent = 6d, while the driver keeps 1s 4d extras plus 2d (25 per cent of the basic 8d).

> Charing Cross to Piccadilly, two men each in two cabs; 8d in each cab; no extras as luggage is carried inside. Owners get aggregate of 1s and the drivers 2d each.

Thus, said *Motor Traction*, the drivers were encouraged to overload their cabs, so wearing out machinery and tyres for which they did not pay.

In 1913 the price of petrol rose sharply, from $6d + 1\frac{1}{2}d$ tax per gallon to $11d + 1\frac{1}{2}d$ tax. This was the contract price, not necessarily the price paid by the public. The increase meant that drivers had to pay 1s 1d per gallon, giving a loss of 1s (5p) per day on average. *Motor Traction*, siding with the drivers for once, pointed out that the taxi driver was the only person who had to pay the government a tax of a shilling in the pound on the whole of his earned income in order to keep his job. The journal suggested a slight increase in the fares, but this was not granted. In January 1913 about 5,000 drivers from most of the major companies went on strike—the smaller firms agreed to charge no more than 8d per gallon, so their drivers, as well as the owner-drivers, remained on the road. The latter did very well, and offset by extra work the higher price they had to pay for petrol. The Fiat Motor Cab Co agreed to sell cabs to their drivers on the instalment payment plan, thus gradually breaking up their large fleet.

The strike lasted for more than two months, but Londoners

were not entirely cab-less, for the owner-driven cabs and those of small operators made up about 40 per cent of the total, and there were, of course, the horse-drawn cabs which reaped a final, though not very spectacular, harvest from their motor rivals. The cab companies offered a compromise price of 10d per gallon, but the drivers wisely refused to pay for their petrol at all, so that in the end the employers were glad to settle for the former price of 8d. This was a victory for the drivers, and it meant, for better or worse, the end of the road for the large fleet owners. The Fiat Co having deliberately broken up their fleet, other firms found themselves forced to do so within the next few years. The first world war undoubtedly hastened the process, but the end would have come anyway. The fleets did not altogether disappear, but there were fewer of them, and from well over a thousand cabs the largest came down to about four hundred.

The decline of the large companies was followed by an increase in the number of owner-drivers. They were, and still are, known in the trade as 'mushes', a word said to be derived from the gold-rush prospectors who were always mushing along in search of gold. The journeyman driver, who works more regular hours, thinks that the owner-driver is similarly devoting his whole life to the search for gold. There had been a few owner-drivers in horse-drawn days, but many more men bought their own cabs from about 1908 onwards. They had the freedom of being their own masters, able to work two days a week or seven according to circumstances or needs, although any taxi driver is a freer man than a lorry or bus driver who has to keep strictly to regular hours and routes. Owner-drivers were among the first to buy motor vehicles on hire purchase as very few had sufficient means to pay out £500 in a lump sum. One of the first companies to offer hire-purchase facilities to cabmen was Mann & Overton, the Unic retailers. The Motor Cab Owner-Drivers' Association was founded in 1910, and found immediate favour with the trade press. *Motor*

Traction considered that owner-driven cabs were invariably smarter and the drivers more courteous than those of journeymen. One Argyll owner, George Stretton of Balham, had such a smart cab that the London agent used to persuade intending purchasers of Argyll private cars to take a ride in it.

In 1911 *Motor Traction* published a report on the financial position of the owner-driver. This showed that the average cab cost £50 to £100 in deposit, plus three annual payments of £150. With day-to-day expenses such as petrol, tyres, repairs and fees for Scotland Yard and London County Council licences (the dual licence was abolished in 1911) annual expenses came to £350. Working about 300 to 310 days per year, meter receipts and tips should make a total income of £495 per annum, giving a profit of £145, or £2 16s per week. This compared favourably with the journeyman's average earnings of £2 2s per week. A good touring job for the summer could improve the situation greatly for the owner-driver but, on the other hand, if the cab were off the road for any length of time, the drain on his resources would be serious. An insurance policy to cover this was being considered by the Owner-Drivers' Association. Another problem was that supplies and spare parts could not be obtained as cheaply by the owner-driver as if bought in bulk by a large firm, but again the association came to the rescue by making bulk purchases and re-selling to the driver at nominal profit.

The war brought many problems to drivers as well as to passengers, especially when petrol rationing was introduced. If asked to take a fare too far afield, a driver might run out of fuel, be unable to obtain any from a garage as he did not have an individual petrol licence, and so be forced to abandon his cab with the risk of facing a charge of obstruction. Thus drivers tended to pick and choose their customers, refusing some journeys on the grounds of 'not enough petrol', although such action was, in fact, contrary to their regulations. These said, and still say, that whilst a driver need not stop for a fare when he is hailed, once he has stopped and engaged in conver-sation, he must take that fare anywhere he is asked, within the six-mile limit.

In October 1917 the owners asked for a 50 per cent increase in fares, to 1s for the first mile and 3d for each succeeding quarter-mile. The Home Secretary refused this request, offer-ing instead a 6d initial hiring fee, which would bear most heavily on those taking short journeys. This offer was rejected by the companies, who said it would bring them not more than 6s net profit per day per cab. The drivers, for their part, were opposed to higher fares as they thought that these would result in lower tips. Because of the high cost of petrol and the general difficulties of wartime, they refused to take out their cabs unless they received free petrol. The companies were thus sandwiched between the Home Secretary on one hand and their employees on the other. A few drivers from the larger companies went on strike in November 1917, and many others left the trade to find work in munitions factories. The petrol charge was abolished in 1918 but, as compensa-tion, the owners sought to introduce a 'driving charge' of a halfpenny per mile. This led to another strike, and a court of arbitration subsequently decided that the charge was not justified. The larger companies could not afford to carry on, and many of their thriftier employees became owner-drivers, leaving only the more shiftless element, 'lacking in skill or manners, or both', as *Motor Traction* described them. The British Motor Cab Co was in serious difficulties early in 1918, and said that even if the fare were raised from 8d to 1s per mile, this still would not be enough. The Home Secretary promised that if the company had to abolish the petrol charge to meet the men's demands (as they did) he would allow a charge of 1s per mile, but he did not do so. Over 700 British Motor Cab taxis were idle from February 1918 onwards, and they were still idle when the war ended nine months later. The company turned its premises over to war work, and in

Page 89 (above) Prototype of 1926 Trojan two-seater landaulet cab, known as the 'Jixi'; *(below)* interior of prototype two-seater saloon cab version

Page 90 (above) The Beardmore Mark III 'Hyper' cab of 1929; *(below)* 'Cape cab' body on a 1929 Morris Commercial chassis. Note sliding door and, unusually, a radiator mascot

1919 the cabs were disposed of to owner-drivers.

Another thorn in the flesh of the wartime taxi driver was the station toll. When the railway companies relaxed their rule against motor cabs in stations, they instituted a toll of 1d to be paid by the driver for the privilege of plying for hire inside the station. This the drivers grudgingly paid but when, in August 1917, the railway companies increased the charge to 2d, the drivers revolted and refused to enter the stations. The public did not suffer unduly as the war had made them used to travelling with smaller amounts of luggage, and they could usually persuade a porter to hail a taxi that 'just happened to be passing outside'. The one penny toll finally ceased to be levied in December 1917.

All these problems, when added to the stress and anxiety which everyone suffered in wartime, combined to exacerbate relations between taxi drivers and the public. Each came to regard the other as an enemy, and unpleasant incidents occurred almost daily. In one of the worst a taxi driver refused to accept a wounded officer, and when the latter tried to enter the cab he was dragged some twenty yards, after which the driver got out and violently assaulted the unfortunate man. Rather than dwell on such episodes, though, one should regard driver/passenger relations as one of the casualties of war which were restored after a few years of peace, and it is a measure of the inherent good nature of the present generation of London taxi drivers that two major events of their year have for long been a London Taxi Trades outing for the war disabled, when Chelsea Pensioners and others are taken by taxis for a day's outing, and a similar excursion, the Norwood Annual Outing, when cab drivers combine to give underprivileged children the pleasure of a day at the seaside.

F

CHAPTER FIVE

TAXICABS BETWEEN THE WARS

Immediately after World War I the taxi situation became worse rather than better, as no new cabs appeared, while the armistice and general celebrations of victory brought a greatly increased demand, especially at night. One well-known restaurant provided all drivers taking up fares after a certain hour with a free supper. Practically all the larger taxi companies were out of business; owner-drivers and small companies were still around, but there were only one-third of the number of cabs on the streets compared with 1914. Large numbers were idle in garages, returned soldiers wanted work, but without suitable financial arrangements the cabs and their potential drivers could not be brought together. However, in April 1919 the British Motor Cab Co began to sell completely overhauled and reconditioned Renault cabs for £180, or £200 on hire-purchase. These prices included the meter and all necessary licences—driving licence, road fund licence and hackney-carriage licence. A large stock of spare parts was also kept. The scheme was aimed particularly at the ex-serviceman who wanted to become an owner-driver, but the cabs were advertised as being useful also to the private motorist who wanted a not-too-powerful landaulet at a reasonable price. New private cars were almost as scarce in 1919 as new taxicabs.

The first post-war announcement of a cab design appeared in *The Times* in April 1919. It read:

Taxicabs—financial co-operation is invited by well-known engineer and designer to build and operate in London and other centres an entirely new Thermo-electric type. Great efficiency, more mileage, suitable for lady drivers, silent working, graceful lines and appearance. Principals or solicitors only.

There were no photographs or further details, and the proposition seems to have had little more substance than the 'chariot' advertised in *The Daily Courant* in 1711. A much more significant announcement of 1919 was that of the new taxicab built by Beardmore Motors Ltd of Paisley, Scotland. Beardmore had one of the most extensive engineering works in the world; among other products they were famous for boilers, aero-engines and complete aircraft. Their taxicabs were built in the Underwood works at Paisley, which had been occupied before the war by the Arrol-Johnston Car Co, while Beardmore passenger cars, which never achieved the fame of their taxicabs, were made in another factory at Anniesland, Glasgow.

The cab had a four-cylinder engine of 2,409cc, rated at 15.6hp, a detachable cylinder head and five-bearing crank-shaft, leather cone clutch and four-speed gearbox. The frame was dropped at the centre so as to allow a reasonably low entrance, even with the mandatory 10in ground clearance. The Beardmore's price was £650 complete, £680 with electric lighting, and £690 with electric lighting and starting. Deliveries began late in 1919 and Beardmores soon became among the most familiar cabs on the streets of London, and many provincial cities as well. The company was the first to make a serious study of the requirements of the taxi trade, as opposed to simply modifying a passenger-car design. From 1923 onwards they kept careful records at service depots, and as a result of these made gradual improvements in design. (Pictures, pp71-2.) One of the first chassis was fitted with a four-seater touring body and used as a test-bed for all modifications to the production chassis. It covered thousands of miles on Highland roads, where its 25ft turning circle coped easily with hairpin bends, until it was retired to become a works hack in 1923.

At the 1920 Commercial Motor Show at Olympia four makers exhibited taxicab chassis: Beardmore, Belsize, Fiat and Unic. The Belsize and the Unic were generally similar to their pre-war models, although the latter sported the V-radiator which was fashionable on many private cars at that time (picture, p71). The Fiat Model 1T was designed wholly for taxicab work, although it was powered by the same 1,846cc side-valve four-cylinder engine that had been used in the pre-war Tipo Zero cars. This developed 18bhp and gave a top speed of 34 to 36mph. Made from 1920 to 1922, the Fiat 1T was one of the few London taxicabs to have disc wheels. It was succeeded by the taxi version of Fiat's mass-production private car, the Tipo 501, but this was never used in London. The next Fiat model to see taxi service in the capital was the 600-based Multipla, which was used by one of the first mini-cab companies in 1961. Another taxi of 1920 was the A.M.L., a new make built by Associated Motors Ltd, of Fernhead Road, Maida Vale, London. It was an assembled vehicle using a French-built Chapuis-Dornier engine of 2,297cc, developing $27\frac{1}{2}$bhp at 2,000rpm. It had a Rolls-Royce type radiator, and a dropped frame similar to that of the Beardmore. The A.M.L. was listed for three seasons but was never exhibited at the shows, and few were made.

Other new makes appeared in London during the 1920s, including the Mepward, Hayes and Yellow Cab. The Mepward was a short-lived and unloved assembled cab powered by a 2,178cc four-cylinder engine. Not more than twelve were built, in 1922, and they were described as noisy and crude by those who drove them. The Hayes was a Canadian product built by the Hayes Wheel Co of Ontario. It was powered by an American-made Continental engine of 2.4 litres capacity, and carried a British-built body. Introduced in 1925 by W. Watson & Co (who later sold the Morris-Commercial cab), the

Hayes sold for £425 complete. This was considerably cheaper than the Beardmore or Unic, both of which cost £625 at that time. *Motor Transport* said 'it should find a ready sale', but though a number were sold between 1925 and 1928 it never became as familiar as the Beardmore or Unic.

The Yellow Cab hailed from Chicago, where the Yellow Cab Manufacturing Co had been building taxicabs since 1915. Mr John Hertz, president of Yellow Cab, spent several months in Europe studying conditions, and as a result decided to introduce Yellow Cabs in both Paris and London. An English subsidiary, the Yellow Cab Manufacturing Co of England Ltd, was set up with a member of parliament, Brigadier E. L. Spears, on the board. His presence may have gone some way to allay fears that Mr Hertz was going to take over the London cab trade in the way he had already done in Chicago. In fact, the Yellow Cab Co never operated the cabs themselves. They were assembled in Acton by the Turpin Engineering Co, and operated by W. & G. du Cros, whose fleet of pre-war Napiers and Panhards was clearly in need of replacement. In 1922 du Cros had announced that they were to introduce a French-built Talbot-Darracq cab with English body. This would have been convenient as the Sunbeam-Talbot-Darracq group which owned Darracq had also recently absorbed W. & G. du Cros, but the Darracq cabs never appeared. The Yellow Cab fleet, which began to appear on the streets towards the end of 1923, consisted of about a hundred vehicles whose canary yellow colour stood out on any rank. They had four-cylinder Continental engines of either 15.9hp or 18.3hp. The drivers wore a grey uniform with a peaked cap and leather leggings. No Yellow Cabs were sold to private owners.

Late in 1923 there appeared in London the first Citroën cabs from the famous French firm which had begun to produce cars only four years previously. The 11.4hp Citroën cab used the same engine as in the firm's private cars and Citroën-Kegresse half-track vehicles, but the chassis was specially designed. The main frame was swept up over the rear axle, and there were double quarter-elliptic springs at the rear. To conform to Scotland Yard regulations, the steering was modified from private-car practice; the drop-arm was inside the frame instead of outside, and the pull-and-push rod, instead of lying more or less parallel with the frame, was taken obliquely over the spring and connected to the stub axle. A central handbrake and gearchange allowed for a door on the driver's side, so that he did not have to scramble over the passengers' luggage, as on earlier cabs. The price was £540, or £595 on hire purchase—£50 deposit and forty-five monthly payments of £12. This brought it between the Beardmore and the Hayes in price, although the Citroën was reduced in 1926 to £495. The Citroën agents, Maxwell Monson Ltd, gave driving instruction and took both driver and cab to the Public Carriage Office for licensing.

A large number of Citroëns were bought by the London General Cab Co, and in 1929 this company introduced a Citroën-based cab of their own construction, built at their Brixton premises. It used the 13/30hp Citroën C4 engine of 1,629cc together with a Citroën three-speed gearbox and radiator. The channel steel frame and landaulet body were London General's own design, from the drawing-board of their chief engineer, P. Geldard. A refinement was a Burovox electric communication device by means of which the passenger had only to press a button and speak into a microphone by his shoulder to communicate with the driver. The cabs had low-pressure balloon tyres, and were considerably lower than the earlier Citroëns. They were available for purchase by owner-drivers, although the majority were operated by London General.

These Citroëns were among the first cabs to offer electric headlamps as a standard fitment, although for the sidelamps, oil lighting was still an option. Until the mid-1920s, cab drivers did not generally favour electric lighting because so much time was spent on the rank, or in very slow travelling, that the ordinary car dynamo could not charge the battery effectively. Also, as powerful headlamps were unnecessary for London driving, most cabbies preferred to stick to oil lighting, or oil at the rear and acetylene at the front. In February 1924 the British Lighting and Ignition Co produced a cab lighting set for £18 15s, including the cost of fitting. The dynamo started charging of the battery when the cab was running as slowly as 8mph on top gear, while the 60amp/hour battery ensured long running, even allowing for crawling below 8mph. The sidelamps could be dimmed when the cab was waiting on the rank. At about the same time the firm of C. A. Vandervell produced a set with a dynamo specially designed to produce a constant output at varying speeds. The equipment included two headlamps, two sidelamps, tail-lamp, interior roof lamp and taximeter lamp. The latter was fitted with the blue glass by which C. A. V.-lit cabs could always be distinguished.

Up to 1929 the appearance of London taxicabs was very high, boxy and old-fashioned, and caused increasingly unfavourable comment as other cars became lower and more sleek. The trade press, in particular, drew comparisons with the modern-looking taxis with front-wheel brakes which were then coming onto the streets of Paris. But French designers did not have to work within the strict limits laid down by the Public Carriage Office which, among other things, forbade front-wheel brakes on the grounds that sudden stops might cause accidents, and would encourage cabbies to drive faster than was necessary or desirable. This rule was not relaxed until 1929.

The greatest problem facing British designers was that of building a comfortable and roomy body on a chassis with an overall length of not more than 14ft and a turning circle of not more than 25ft. This accounted for the upright, front-heavy appearance of most cabs of the 1920s. The minimum inside height of 40in made graceful lines impossible, while the turning circle necessitated a wheelbase shorter than many light cars with engines of half the taxicab's capacity. These problems, combined with the small market, explain why so few firms went in for the manufacture of taxis. In 1927 a committee was set up to enquire into the high cost of taxicabs, and found that lack of competition among manufacturers was the chief reason. It is significant that between 1918 and 1929 no large British manufacturer entered the taxi business. With the appearance on the scene of Morris in 1929 and Austin in 1930 a new era of taxi manufacture began, and the latter make soon came to dominate the trade.

Turning to the design of cabs, the 1927 committee made a number of recommendations, the most important of which were the following:

   (i) The minimum ground clearance should be reduced from 10in to 7in.
  (ii) The minimum turning circle should be increased from 25ft to 40ft.
 (iii) A suitable dashboard fuel tank should be permitted.
  (iv) Advertisements should be permitted inside taxis, but not outside.

Police Superintendent Claro of Scotland Yard agreed with all recommendations except that on the turning circle, and the Home Secretary agreed to recommendations (i) and (iv). The former led to new, lower cabs appearing in 1929 and 1930. Designers were encouraged to break out of their stagnation and to produce the best crop of new cabs ever seen. There was no major taxi builder who did not bring out a new design between 1928 and 1930.

The first to appear was the Morris Commercial, powered by the 15.9hp four-cylinder engine used in the firm's light trucks. Engine and four-speed gearbox were of unit construction, and there was an overhead worm rear axle, as on other Morris Commercial products. Refinements included microphone communication with the driver, a door-controlled roof-light and blinds fitted to the rear quarter windows. There was accommodation for luggage on a roof rack, as well as in the traditional position beside the driver. Although it was the first of the 'new generation' of cabs the Morris Commercial still had a number of old-fashioned features, such as no side screen for the driver and rear-wheel brakes only. Both of these shortcomings were due to Scotland Yard regulations and not to the designer. The price was a moderate £395 complete. The cabs were distributed, not by the normal Morris outlets, but through a new and separate concern, the International Taxicab Co of Sheffield, headed by the well-known motor trader, George Kenning. Later, Morris Commercial cabs were distributed by William Watson & Co of Liverpool, Mr Watson being a personal friend of William Morris, later Lord Nuffield. In June 1929 a Morris Commercial hire car was added to the range, with four doors and a full-width two-piece windscreen in place of the three-quarter screen of the cab. At least one Morris Commercial cab was fitted experimentally with a single overhead camshaft Wolseley engine, and a split radiator cooling both water and oil. This ran, in provincial service, until some years after the second world war.

In May 1929 Beardmore announced their 'Hyper' model. This had an engine of smaller bore than the previous models, 72mm compared with 80mm, giving an RAC horsepower rating of 12.8 compared with 15.9. In the days when tax was paid on horsepower at a rate of £1 per hp, this was a useful gain for the fleet owner. The 1,954cc engine was a monobloc unit, there was a four-speed gearbox and, for the first time on a London cab, four-wheel brakes (picture, p90). The 'Hyper' was six inches lower than its predecessors and had improved steering. One of the drawbacks of the earlier Beardmores had been their very heavy steering which made driving for long periods extremely tiring. This drawback also applied to the operation of clutch and brakes.

In July 1929 the previously-mentioned Citroën-based London General cab appeared, and in October Austin entered the trade with a taxicab based on their 'Twelve-Four' chassis. Two body styles were originally offered, a landaulet and a four-light saloon, both made by the Elkington Carriage Co of Chiswick. Prices were £375 for the landaulet and £395 for the saloon. These, and other cab prices of the period, do not represent such a bargain compared with those of the early 1920s as might appear, for all prices, and incomes too, were lower at this time. Initially, the Austin was not licensed for London as its turning circle was too great. It was used in Manchester and other provincial cities, and in April 1930, after consultation with Mann & Overton, the design was modified to make it suitable for London. The alterations included a different front axle with rod-operated brakes, whereas the provincial model had used cables. The steering column became more upright and there was no front door on the near side. (picture, p107.) The appearance of this conventional cab caused no particular excitement in the press or anywhere else, but within a few years Austin was to become the predominant make of taxi on the London streets, a position they still hold and are likely to hold for the foreseeable future.

Fifth of the new generation of London taxis was the revised Unic. Imports of the old-style Unic had dropped sharply during the 1920s, and in 1928 a new company, Unic Motors (1928) Ltd, was formed with premises at Cricklewood, North London. They began by importing lorry chassis from France, and in July 1930 they introduced their new taxicab, designed and assembled in London although using the French-built engine. Known as the KF1, the new cab had a two-litre side-valve engine and a low chassis with curved cross-members passing below the propeller shaft. The wheelbase was longer than most cabs at 9ft 6in and the interior of the landaulet body was exceptionally roomy. As on most of the new cabs, there was electric telephone communication between passengers and driver. Despite these attractions, the KF1 was less reliable and therefore less popular than the old Unics and manufacture lasted for only three years. Fewer than one hundred were made, but there were one or two still in service as late as 1951.

An interesting design which appeared in 1929 was the Cape cab body. This was the brainchild of Mr W. Gowan from Cape Town, South Africa, hence its name. It had no side-facing doors, instead the passengers entered by a door which slid across the chassis frame immediately behind the luggage area. This avoided the danger of an open door hitting pedestrians or obstructions on the pavement. The body had oval side and rear windows, and the prototype was for two passengers, although the inventor said that provision could be made for four. The driver was isolated on a bucket seat with no off-side door or screen, and must have found his position very draughty. However, *The Commercial Motor* said 'It gives complete privacy for those in the interior of the vehicle, and in countries where the racial colour problem exists, this may be of some importance.' (Picture, p.90). The prototype, built on a Morris Commercial chassis, was licensed by Scotland Yard and tested on London streets. In 1933, a modified form of the Cape cab was also licensed, and about twenty Austins so fitted went into service.

Alongside all these new designs there were still lingering pre-war cabs such as Napiers, Panhards, and the two-cylinder Renaults. These had been the subject of criticism as early as 1922. *The Daily Mail* had complained of the unfairness of having to pay the same rate for antiquated two-cylinder cabs as for the excellent four-cylinder cabs on the roads. The same journey took ten minutes by modern cab, fifteen minutes by a venerable two-cylinder cab of 1909 vintage. In Paris, old cabs charged a lower rate, and when the new four-cylinder Renaults came onto the streets the owners were so proud of them that they put large notices on the back reading: '*Nou-*

veau taxi à quatre cylindres'. London papers were eager to condemn the old taxis; one wrote of 'the decaying vehicle of which the engine, threatening to surrender its poor ghost at any moment, wheezes and groans its way from gear to gear with a fierce clutch that jerks the passenger from his uneasy seat on decrepit upholstery resting on springs as weary as itself.' They remarked that it was often difficult to detect these antiques because of false bonnets and a little paint. Five years later, in 1927, the press was still having a field-day at the expense of old cabs, saying that some of them would make a most impressive Chamber of Horrors for the re-built waxworks exhibition of Madame Tussaud's. The Marquess of Donegal, writing in *The Sunday News* in October 1927, said that there were between a hundred and two hundred twenty-one-year old cabs in London. This was clearly an exaggeration as there were fewer than a hundred cabs in all at the end of 1906. The illustration to his article showed a decrepit Charron of about 1914.

One way of eliminating the older cabs was to have a stricter annual test, or even to ban cabs of over a certain age. The authorities were unwilling to do this, however, as so many old cabs were the sole livelihood of their owners. The test was not, in fact, very stringent. It was conducted with an empty cab which was required to reach not less than 20mph on the level, and 6mph up a gradient. Drivers were given a chance to tune up their cabs before the test. From time to time members of parliament pressed for laws against old cabs, but on each occasion they received a similar answer, from either the Home Secretary or the Minister of Transport. This was to the effect that as all taxis had to pass a fitness test there was no point in discriminating against old ones simply on grounds of age or antique appearance. After all, in the early 1930s there were still some growlers and one or two hansoms around. However, in August 1933 it was announced that all cabs of fifteen years' service were gradually to be withdrawn, and the useful life of a cab was to be reduced in stages to ten years. This plan was frustrated by the second world war, but was re-established with the disappearance of the last pre-war cabs in 1955. There is, in fact, no law against a cab more than ten years old continuing in service, but the special test involved is so stringent that it would be uneconomic to spend the necessary money on preparing the cab for it.

London's taxi population never regained its five-figure level of pre-1914 days, varying between 7,900 and 8,200 during the inter-war years. There were considerably more drivers than cabs, as one cab would often have one driver for day work and another for nights. Sometimes, two owner-drivers would club together to buy a cab and then 'double it', as the principle of day and night was called. The big fleet owners had mostly disappeared, but the London General Cab Co still maintained 550 cabs in 1931; 320 Citroëns and 230 of their own make. In order to attract night drivers, they started a free bus service covering six routes to take drivers home from their headquarters at Brixton between the hours of 1.0am and 4.0am. The service was operated by a twenty-seater Chevrolet with a body built on the company's premises. As a result of this service, some day drivers turned to night work, with increased earnings to themselves and their company. Other progressive ideas operated by London General included a group insurance scheme and free legal advice and aid when needed.

Cab driving between the wars was an uncertain business compared with today, as there were more cabs on the road and far fewer potential fares; working-class taxi riders were still almost non-existent. Ranks were full to capacity, and a driver might spend several hours waiting, or looking, for work. Railway stations were certain sources of work, although a long wait might be necessary. Waterloo had its 'Rats' Hole' under the station where up to a hundred cabs could wait, and frequently did when a boat train was expected. Jack Cohen remembers waiting there for six hours for the train from the Queen Mary's maiden voyage. At Liverpool Street, drivers would turn up at 5.30am to wait for the Harwich boat train, due in at 8.30.

Taxi drivers have always been a difficult body of men to organise into societies, but an attempt was made in 1921 with the National Federation of Hackney Carriage Proprietors. The journal of this federation was called *Steering Wheel* and, although the federation broke up in 1926, the magazine flourished and has become the leading organ of the cab trade. In its golden anniversary issue of 25 December 1971, it carried congratulations from Her Majesty the Queen, the Home Secretary, the Leader of the Opposition, and numerous theatrical and sporting personalities including Sir Alec Guinness, Sir Ralph Richardson, Harry Secombe, Jimmy Saville, and Henry Cooper. As well as giving legal and general information to the taxi driver, *Steering Wheel* carries regular reviews of plays and occasional articles on subjects such as Wren's churches, all aimed at encouraging the driver to help his fares to enjoy London. No other trade journal has rivalled *Steering Wheel*, although there was a short-lived monthly, *Taxi World*, published by the Taxi Drivers' League in the 1930s. Both league and journal collapsed after about six years. More recently, the Licensed Taxi Drivers' Association has published its own journal (see page 145).

After the flood of new models at the beginning of the decade, the 1930s were a period of consolidation and gradual improvement rather than innovation in taxicab design. The original Austin Twelve, nicknamed the 'Grand Piano' or 'Upright Grand,' was modified in 1932 by the introduction of synchromesh between third and top gears, becoming known as the 'Twin Top,' or TT model. (Picture, p108). In 1934 a further modification was the adoption of a worm-drive rear axle which enabled a lower body to be fitted, while still keeping a completely flat floor in the passenger compartment.

The most expensive private cars might have a propeller shaft 'hump', but not a London taxi. This model became known as the 'Low Loader' or 'LL', and so its predecessors came to be called 'High Loaders' or 'HLs', although they were never so called when new.

The 'LL' was made from 1934 to mid-1938, when it received a complete facelift. The vertical vintage-style radiator was replaced by a narrow, sloping grille borrowed from Austin's private cars, the rear of the body was inclined instead of vertical, and contemporary styling features, such as skirted mudguards and horizontal bonnet louvres, appeared. Drivers nicknamed the new Austin the 'Flash Job', but despite its appearance it was mechanically unchanged from its predecessors. The 1,861cc Twelve Four engine was the same as had been used in the 1930 cab and the wheelbase of 9ft 4in was also unaltered. The 'Flash Job' was the last pre-war Austin taxi, and remained in production until the outbreak of war in September 1939. A very small number of cabs were delivered up to January 1940, and about 400 already completed chassis were acquired by the Army, fitted with light truck bodies, and used for driving instruction. At the end of the war in 1945, about 300 were bought back by Mann & Overton and dismantled for spares.

Like the Rolls-Royce of the 1930s, all Austin cabs had coachbuilt bodies by outside firms. Elkington of Chiswick were responsible for the original model, but the bulk of 1930s production was by three firms, Jones of Westbourne Grove, Strachan of Acton, and Vincents of Reading. In addition, two fleet operators, Birch Brothers of Kentish Town, and Goode & Cooper of Brixton, made a few bodies for their own cabs and for other operators. Other smaller coachbuilders included Ricketts, and Christopher Dodson. An unusual sight in the early 1930s was the so-called 'Chinese Austin'. These were operated by the London General Cab Co, and used bodies taken from the company's old Citroëns and mounted on new Austin chassis. A total of 196 of these hybrids were made.

Practically all Austins carried landaulet bodies, the rear portion of which could be opened in summer. There were two kinds, the single landaulet with only two windows in the passenger compartment, and the rarer three-quarter landaulet with small 'quarter lights' behind the main windows. (See pictures, pp108 and 125). The landaulet style dated back to earliest days of motoring but was almost extinct on the private car by 1939. From 1936, some Jones bodies had a swept tail, known as the fishtail. At £400 for the complete cab, they were £5 more expensive than the Vincent or Strachan cabs.

A total of 5,850 Austin cabs were sold in London between April 1930 and the end of 1938, and during this time the make established itself as the leader of the trade. The following table will give an idea of their relative position. 'Other makes' were Beardmore and Morris Commercial, together with a few Unic KFls up to 1933 only.

New Registrations	Austin	Other Makes
1930	271	269
1931	400	243
1932	309	204
1933	834	128
1934	1,Ⅱ1	302
1935	1,178	337
1936	875	307
1937	659	96
1938	213	85

Beardmore's staple production was the 'Hyper' until the end of 1933, when it was replaced by the Mark IV Paramount. Scottish production ceased, and all subsequent Beardmores were built in the firm's new factory at Hendon, in north-west London. The Paramount was a cheaper vehicle than the 'Hyper', with a 13.9hp, 1,944cc four-cylinder Commer engine developing 48bhp. It had a new chassis with cruciform bracing, and was offered with a choice of four body styles: single landaulet, three-quarter landaulet, four-light

Page 107 (above) London's first Austin taxi, the Elkington-bodied Twelve-Four of 1930; *(below)* a Morris Commercial Junior Six cab of 1934

Page 108
(top)
1933 Austin TT
with Strachan
single landaulet
body;

(middle)
1936 Austin LL
with Strachan
single landaulet
body;

(bottom)
1937 Austin LL
with Jones 'fishtail'
three-quarter
landaulet body

saloon and six-light saloon. Unlike Austin, Beardmore built their own bodies. The Paramount was gradually improved during the 1930s, the Mark V of 1936 having a longer wheelbase of 9ft 6in compared with 9ft 0in of previous models, and a lower appearance. The last pre-war Beardmore was the Mark VI, introduced at the end of 1937. It was similar to the Mark V, but had synchromesh on all four gears. The price was considerably higher than that of the Austin; £480 for a single landaulet and £485 for a three-quarter landaulet.

Morris Commercial cabs were made in small numbers throughout the period. The large four-cylinder engine of the original International cab gave way in 1932 to a smaller 13.9 hp unit, and in August 1934 Morris introduced London's first six-cylinder cab, the 15hp, 1,938cc Junior Six. It sold for a modest £385 and, like its contemporaries, came in single and three-quarter landaulet models. From 1937 to 1939 the G2, as the cab was now called, used the slightly smaller six-cylinder engine of the Morris Fourteen-Six car, of 14.06hp and 1,818cc. Only the single landaulet style was listed, the price still being £385.

With only three firms in production and the older cabs disappearing rapidly, there was much less variety in London taxis by the late 1930s. Ford built one experimental cab in 1936, with a specially-designed limousine body on a standard 22hp V-8 chassis, but it was never licensed by Scotland Yard. Unless some radical changes had been made to its steering geometry, it would hardly have satisfied the turning circle requirements, for the standard Ford V-8 required 40ft, compared with the 25ft of the Scotland Yard rules. Some of the regulations were still archaic by modern car standards. From 1930 onwards, the driver was allowed a complete windscreen to shield him from wind and rain, but his left-hand side was completely exposed and until 1938 he was allowed no window on his right-hand door.

G

CHAPTER SIX

FOUR SEATS GOOD,
TWO SEATS BAD

A curious episode not touched upon in the last chapter was that of the two-seater cabs. The first taxis had been strictly for two passengers only, being virtually motorised hansoms, but by 1910 the four-seater with two forward-facing seats and two rear-facing occasionals, had become the norm. The only pre-war attempt to revive the two-seater was made by Frank Morriss, an ingenious motor trader and engineer who had been car repairer to King Edward VII at Sandringham, and later experimented with steam cars. In 1914 he proposed to import Twombly cyclecars from the United States, and fit them with two-seater bodies for London use. Unfortunately, the Twombly Car Co of Nutley, New Jersey, went out of business in 1915, and although Morriss imported other American cars after the war, he played no further part in the history of the taxicab. A two-seater landaulet based on the Model 'T' Ford was rumoured to be around London during the spring of 1919, but nothing came of it.

At the 1920 Olympia Motorcycle Show a number of sidecar taxis were exhibited by such well-known motorcycle makers as Campion, Rex, B.S.A. and Excelsior. The Campion seated two passengers side by side, while the Rex had staggered seating. The first of these new taxis went into service in Glasgow in December 1920, charging fares 33 per cent lower than those of ordinary taxis. The following year Nottingham acquired a fleet of Campions, and sidecar taxis were also seen in Birmingham, Bradford, Leeds, Margate and Brighton. In March 1920 London taxicab fares had been increased to 1s per mile (see Appendix Four) and, inevitably, people began to ask why London could not have similar small taxis at lower rates. The Ministry of Transport referred the question to a departmental committee. In their report of January 1921 the committee rejected the idea largely on the grounds of safety —one of the requirements of a London taxi was that it should be better able to withstand an accident than a private car, and this the flimsy sidecar clearly could not do. In fact, the sidecar taxi did not last long in provincial service, and it was probably no loss to Londoners that they never reached the metropolis.

The two-seater, four-wheeled taxicab was another matter, however, and there were many sound arguments in its favour. Early in 1924 a Morris Cowley with two-seater cab body was licensed for use in Oxford, while Birmingham had a fleet of 10.8hp Clynos with two-seater landaulet bodies in 1925. In April of that year the Home Secretary, Sir William Joynson-Hicks, appointed a committee to look into the question of two-seaters for London. The committee called seventeen witnesses, including representatives of manufacturers, the cab trade and the licensing authority. The case in favour of two-seaters was put most strongly by R. W. Owen, a director of White, Holmes & Co, one of the firms who were building prototype two-seater cabs (the K.R.C.). His, and other, advocates' arguments can be summarised as follows:

> The cab trade was in a bad way at the time, due to high fares keeping potential cab-riders away. It was impossible to run a four-seater profitably on a fare of less than 1s per mile, but a two-seater could make more profit at 9d than a four-seater at 1s, as well as giving drivers a commission of 40 per cent instead of 33 per cent as at present. This was because the two-seater would save on original purchase price, fuel, oil and tyres.

Four-seaters were seldom filled to capacity. It was estimated that only about 10 per cent of hirings involved more than two persons. Thus their engines and chassis were constructed for a load heavier than that which they habitually carried. In the lorry and bus world, this would be regarded as very bad economics, yet it had been tolerated in the cab trade for years.

Cheaper cabs would encourage the taxi habit in those who had not used them before, to the good of the whole trade.

The cab trade's representatives were unanimously against the idea of the two-seater, their main arguments being as follows:

Taxis were only working three hours out of ten, so more cabs would make the situation worse.

More taxis would increase the already serious problem of traffic congestion.

If there were cabs at two fare rates on the same rank, the principle of hiring the leading cab would have to go. (It was pointed out to the committee by the police that this principle, although generally observed, was not enforceable by law; the hirer had the right to choose any cab on the rank.)

Lower rates for new cabs would threaten the existing four-seaters. If they took a lot of the latter's trade, it would be especially hard on owner-drivers who had bought cabs on hire-purchase and were still paying for them.

The introduction of differential fares would tend to force all fares down, to the obvious detriment of trade, both for owner-drivers and fleet operators.

An interesting exception to the opposition to lower fares, though not to two-seaters, came from the Owner Drivers League, formed by H. J. Dunn. In a pamphlet sent to owner-drivers, Mr Dunn introduced his cause thus:

In the *Sunday Express* of the 17th of May 1925 there is an article headed 'The Taxi Gondola in London'. There is only one place for a Taxi Gondola in London—the Thames! Owner Drivers, do you realise your strength? You can not only stop the Two-Seater, but drive all cabs not owner-driven off the streets. Owner Drivers, 'for the love of Mike', wake up! Fight for your own! Think, who can and do own cabs today? Join the Owner Drivers League and broom this lot out! Make the Cab Trade what it should be—an Owner Driver's job. You are strong enough if you organise! Join the Owner Drivers League and do it. Have you forgotten 1913? If you have, the masters have not. The Two-Seater can crush you! Then the masters will have the journey-men at their own price, and you with them. Don't forget this! It is life or death with you. Join the Owner Drivers League and live!

In the rest of his pamphlet Mr Dunn detailed the evidence he had given before the committee. He claimed that fleet owners wanted the two-seater to come, and that if the owners ran two-seaters at a cheaper rate, then the owner-drivers with four-seaters at, inevitably, a more expensive rate, would be put out of business and forced to join the large firms, thus restoring the position of pre-1914 days. To counteract this, Mr Dunn suggested an overall reduction of fares by 50 per cent; this, he claimed, would result in a 200 per cent increase in trade. This would not bring increased hours of work, but would merely mean that the cab would be earning its keep for 90 per cent of its running time, instead of 30 per cent as at present.

Representatives of the Motor Cab Trade Protection Society, the Motor Cab Owner Drivers' Association and the Transport & General Workers' Union told the committee that they were prepared to consider some reduction after the first mile, but not on the initial charge. The committee, in its turn, said that the convenience of the public must be considered before any questions of hardship or vested interests, and that if a cheaper service was offered, it should not be denied. This seems a curious and unenlightened attitude when one com-pares the inconvenience to a small section of the public of paying for a larger taxi than they might want, with the hard-ship of a driver losing his living. Nevertheless, the committee did have a number of reservations about the problems raised on cab ranks by differential fares. Although not objecting in principle to two-seaters, they thought that a two-level fare structure was undesirable. Their recommendations were:

(i) That it is not desirable that the Home Secretary should make an Order (as he is empowered to do) which would prohibit

the licensing of a vehicle which complies with Scotland Yard
requirements on the sole grounds that it is constructed to carry
fewer than four passengers.

(ii) That the public convenience is best served by the one
standard rate of fares.

(iii) That the Home Secretary should call a conference of the
cab trade with a view to securing an agreed reduction in existing
fares applicable to all types of taxis.

(iv) That in the absence of any agreement for a uniform fare
for two passengers, the following fares should be fixed for the
two-seater: initial hiring, 9d per mile, and for each subsequent
third of a mile, 3d. Waiting time at the rate of 4s per hour.

In a minority report, Mr R. C. Morrison, MP, did not agree
with recommendations (i) and (iii) which, he thought, might
result in increasing the number of taxicabs and so adding to
the congestion of traffic. He thought that no steps should be
taken to license two-seater cabs until the Home Secretary had
obtained power to limit the total number of cabs plying for
hire. This suggestion has been made at various times before
and since, but has never been put into effect.

The report was published in August 1925, but before then
several other interests not represented on the committee had
had their say. Mr E. S. Shrapnell-Smith of the Commercial
Motor Users' Association feared that, as two-seaters were
cheaper to operate, the four-seaters would eventually disappear altogether, and this would lead to overcrowding when
four passengers did want to be carried. He thought a possible
alternative to the four-seater would be a single-seater. This
would be so much smaller as to be no competition to the conventional cab and yet would find favour with many businessmen and others travelling on their own. In Paris, a number of
Peugeot 'Monoplace' taxis were in service, with narrow bodies
in which the passenger sat in tandem behind the driver. They
plied only between 7.0am and 10.0pm, and not at all on Sun-
days. The initial charge was 70 centimes compared with 1
franc for larger cabs. Paris also had two-seaters, but these
charged the same fare as full-sized cabs.

Although empowered to license two-seater cabs in August 1925, the Home Secretary, Sir William Joynson-Hicks, did not in fact do so until April 1926. The press, who had already christened the new cabs 'Jixis', after the Home Secretary's nickname 'Jix', eagerly prophesied that there would be 500 of them on the London streets by the autumn. Regulations for the two-seaters were issued, of which the salient details are given below:

	Two-seater	Four-seater
Minimum clearance	8in	10in
,, track	48in	52in
,, tyre diameter	760mm	810mm
Maximum length	14ft	14ft
,, breadth	5ft 9in	5ft 9in

The fare was fixed at 9d per mile, thus ignoring item (ii) of the committee's recommendations that there should be only one rate of fare. However, a minister always has the right to over-rule a committee's recommendations, as was shown in the recent case of the Roskill Commission's report on London's third airport.

Before any 'Jixis' could appear, somebody had to make them, and the first company to offer one for licensing was the small firm of White, Holmes & Co of King Street, Hammersmith. They were not newcomers to the cab trade, for their predecessors, the National Motor Cab Co, had run a fleet of Unics before the war (see p64). Their product was called the K.R.C. after the designers, Kingston, Richardson and Crutchley, and a number of light cars were sold under this name before the taxi appeared. This had a 9.8hp four-cylinder Coventry-Climax engine of 1,246cc capacity. The landaulet body was six inches shorter, twelve inches narrower and eight inches lower than that of the standard cab, but the driver's accommodation was the same, that is forty-two inches from dashboard to back of seat. The price complete was £500, or £200 less than a Beardmore four-seater.

The K.R.C. was announced in May 1925, and one was

licensed by Scotland Yard and running on test during the summer. London cabbies were predictably sarcastic when they saw it; 'Oh how nice, a penny a mile we presume?', and 'It'll last a week on the road, you wait and see', were among the politer remarks made. A number of K.R.C. two-seaters did run in Harrogate, in Yorkshire, but they never went into London service. In 1926 the makers were asked if they could mass-produce their cab, but they were unable to do so 'because of the present dislocation of industry', the aftermath of the recent general strike.

White, Holmes & Co were, in any event, a very small concern, whereas two other firms to submit 'Jixi' designs were considerably more substantial. One was Trojan, who were at that time backed by Leyland Motors Ltd, and were already well-known for their solid-tyred cars and vans. They had built fifty solid-tyred saloon taxis for use in Tokyo in 1924, but their 'Jixi' of 1926 ran on pneumatics and had either a saloon or landaulet body. Probably not more than two prototypes were built. (Pictures, p89.) The other two-seater came from the French firm of Berliet, famous for cars and trucks since the turn of the century. Their cab was based on their 10/20hp car chassis, many of which were used for taxi work in their native Lyons and other French cities. (Picture, p72.) It was provisionally passed for London use by Scotland Yard in March 1927, and it was said that up to 200 per month would be put on the streets during the summer. In the *Daily Express* for 4 April there appeared the following advertisement in the 'Situations Vacant' column:

> Motor drivers to train for two-seater taxicabs: liberal payment: must be physically sound, energetic, good appearance and well-experienced drivers. Send full particulars to Box 320.

It is not certain that this referred to the Berliet company, but it seems more than likely.

However, before any two-seaters could appear, the Home Secretary had a change of heart and, in April, he rescinded the Two-Seater Order in return for the cab trade's agreement to a new schedule of fares. This was 6d for the first two-thirds of a mile (or seven and a half minutes), 3d for each subsequent one-third (or three and three-quarter minutes), 6d for each extra passenger above two, and 3d per piece of outside luggage. This effectively made the rate 9d per mile, a 25 per cent reduction on the previous rate. The firms who had built two-seaters were understandably perplexed, and Mr R. W. Owen, who had given evidence in favour of two-seaters to the committee of inquiry, said: 'Frankly, I don't believe the Home Secretary will prevent "Jixies" being put on the road. Far too much money and labour have been spent on them.' But for all Mr Owen's optimism, it was not the first or the last time that private money was wasted because of the whim of government, and the two-seaters never did appear.

'Jix' himself, however, was not quite out of trouble, for no sooner had the new fares been fixed than the drivers discovered that the rescinding of the Two-Seater Order applied only to two-seaters at a lower rate of fare, so that, theoretically, they could still legitimately ply for hire if they charged the same rate as a four-seater. This was considered a breach of the Home Secretary's promise, and the Joint Conference of the Cab Trade withdrew its assent to the proposed fare reduction. 'Jix' replied that he was empowered by parliament to fix fares at whatever rate he thought fit, without the consent of anyone. There was much bickering in parliament between the Home Secretary and the taxi interests, after which it was agreed that the new scale should be tried for an experimental period. In the result, it remained in force until 1933, when the initial hiring fee was raised by 3d.

In October 1928 a company called Two-Seater Taxicabs Ltd was formed 'with the intention of manufacturing and dealing in two-seater cabs'. Their products were to be on the streets by early 1929 but, needless to say, they were not. The idea cropped up again a few years later when there was a minor boom in three-wheeled passenger cars. Several makers such as B.S.A., Morgan and Coventry-Victor, were building attractive four-seater three-wheelers, and it was reported in *The Commercial Motor* that one manufacturer had produced a three-wheeled saloon suited to taxi use. Scotland Yard were unwilling to license it but, said *The Commercial Motor*, 'If three-wheeler two-seater taxis become popular in the provinces, their adoption in London should only be a matter of time.' However, the provinces thought the new vehicles too close to the sidecar taxis of ten years before, and they were not adopted. A single-passenger three-wheeler (the 400cc Goliath) was used in some numbers as a taxi in Berlin in 1931, but as far as London was concerned the full-sized cab had no rival until the appearance of the minicab in 1961.

CHAPTER SEVEN

THE POST-WAR TAXICAB

Soon after the outbreak of war in September 1939, the manu-facture of taxicabs ceased and during the next few years London's fleet was drastically reduced in numbers. In 1940, more than 400 cabs were requisitioned and fitted with machine-guns for anti-paratroop patrol work. This was the period when the invasion of Britain was expected daily. Another 2,000 taxis were organised into fire-fighting units. Trailers were bolted onto the chassis and loaded with ladders, axes and stirrup pumps; their high degree of manoevrability and their drivers' intimate knowledge of London often en-abled them to be on the scene of a blaze before the larger fire engines could get there. There were five men to each cab, all of them cabbies unfit for military service, and all were attached to the London Fire Brigade. They wore firemen's uniform, with steel helmets. As was inevitable because of the heavy bombing, far more cabs were destroyed through enemy action than in the first world war, and London's cab fleet was down to under 3,000 by the end of the war in 1945.

The first post-war taxicab to appear was a Nuffield product, the Oxford, or Wolseley Oxford. The prototype of this cab had been placed in service in 1940, and had run throughout the war, covering nearly 100,000 miles. Because of this ex-perience, Wolseley were able to make their production plans as soon as the war ended; an assembly line was laid down at their Ward End, Birmingham, factory during the latter half of 1946 and the first production Oxford taxi came into service in February 1947. This was more than a year before Austin were able to launch their post-war cab, the FX3. The Oxford had a 1,802cc four-cylinder overhead-valve engine and a wide, four-light limousine body. Just as nearly all pre-war cabs were landaulets, so all post-war ones were fixed-head limousines made of pressed steel or aluminium. The craftsmen needed for coachbuilt bodies on ash frames were simply not available after the war. The first Oxfords had no window on the driver's left, but a fully-enclosed cab was introduced in 1948. (Picture, p126.) In 1950 a private-hire version with front door on the nearside and a six-light body became available, and the six-light body was also used on the taxicab.

The pre-war Morris-Commercial cab had been distributed by William Watson & Co in the same way that Mann & Overton sold Austins. After the war, Mr Watson felt that he was too old to continue the business, and it was taken over by Beardmore Motors, who had no post-war cab of their own. About 1,800 Oxfords were sold by Beardmores, but with the Austin-Nuffield merger in 1952 under the banner of the British Motor Corporation, there was no longer room for two taxicabs from the same organisation. Austin's FX3 was the newer design, and so became the sole British Motor Corporation taxicab. Beardmore then returned to making their own cabs, the Mark VII appearing in September 1954.

While Nuffield were getting their first Oxfords on the road, Austin had been experimenting with their own post-war design. The first of these, the FX1 of 1945, used the engine, gearbox and other components from the Austin Twelve car. This was not the same engine that had powered the pre-war cabs, but the Light Twelve Four, a smaller unit of 1,535cc capacity. The old engine, which had first seen the light of day on cars in 1921, is sometimes known as the Heavy Twelve Four, but this is only a retrospective name and was not used at the time. The Light Twelve engine of 1945 developed

40bhp, which proved insufficiently powerful for a 28cwt cab. The FX1 was given a test body, but the generally similar FX2 never progressed beyond the chassis stage, and for the FX3 Austin chose a new engine, the 2,199cc Sixteen, which powered the firm's excellent Sixteen saloon of 1945-9 and the later A70 Hampshire and Hereford saloons, as well as the 25cwt three-way delivery van. This unit developed 52bhp at 3,800rpm, later increased to 56bhp. It was still available as an option on Austin cabs in 1971.

The FX3, which was launched at Mann & Overton's Wandsworth Bridge Road premises in London in June 1948, had a pressed steel body made by Carbodies of Coventry; it was lower and longer than those of pre-war Austins, although the wheelbase was 1¾in shorter. Girling brakes were fitted, with two leading shoes on the front wheels. The driver's cab was fully enclosed, with a sliding partition on his left. The FX3 was the first taxicab to standardise this improvement, although Wolseley quickly adopted it on their Oxford. The luggage platform was still open, and remained so until the introduction of the FX4 in 1958. The only FX3 to have a nearside door was the Hirecar model, introduced in 1950. When it first came out, the FX3 cost £936 1s 8d inclusive of purchase tax, very close to the £933 10s 7d of the Oxford. (Picture, p126.)

The early 1950s were among the worst years the London cab trade had ever undergone. Fuel costs had risen by 83 per cent since 1939, the cost of living by 100 per cent and the price of a new cab by more than 100 per cent, but fares only rose by 66 per cent (9d to 1s 3d per mile basic rate) and then not until 1951. There were just under 8,000 cabs licensed in 1950, but by 1953 this figure had dropped to 5,443 as the pre-war cabs were scrapped and neither owner-drivers nor companies could afford to buy new ones. In 1952, only 132 new cabs were licensed. The trade emerged from these doldrums when a saviour appeared in the form of the small diesel engine.

Diesels had been used on heavy commercial vehicles for over twenty years, and before the war a cabbie had written an article in *The Commercial Motor* saying that an oil-engined taxi would be very welcome. He estimated that a mileage of 36 per gallon could be obtained, compared with 12 to 15 for a petrol engine, and said that the oil engine was less easily stalled, a great advantage in London. An extra £120 in first cost would, he thought, be compensated for by a saving of 50 per cent in running expenses. Unfortunately, there was no home-built oil engine of less than three litres' capacity available, and this was clearly too large for a London taxi. In 1953, however, the Standard Motor Co brought out a two-litre four-cylinder diesel unit adapted from the one used in the Ferguson tractor. The taxi-operators, Birch Brothers of Kentish Town, offered a conversion scheme at a cost of £325 for the new engine and the labour of conversion. The saving in fuel costs was in the region of 35 to 50 per cent and many cabs were converted. Austin introduced a 2.2-litre diesel in September 1954, and by the end of 1955 about 30 per cent of London's taxis were diesel-powered. Initial cost of a diesel-engined FX3 was £942, compared with £847 for a petrol-engined model, but so popular did the diesel become that in 1955 Mann & Overton were selling nine diesels to every one petrol-engined cab. In 1958 Perkins brought out their Four 99 two-litre diesel engine which was installed in the Beardmore and Winchester cabs.

The Austin FX3 remained in production until the end of 1958, by which time 7,267 had been sold for use in London. Several hundred went into provincial use, and it also became the first London-type taxicab to be exported in any numbers. About 700 went abroad during the 1950s, 250 going to Spain and the balance to Sweden, Denmark, Eire, Iran and New Zealand. A number were fitted with van bodies and used for delivery of London newspapers, the first time a taxi chassis had been employed for goods work. Their excellent manoeuvreability combined with a good turn of speed made them very suitable for this kind of work, and their successor, the FX4, was also used for newspaper delivery work.

The third taxi make of the 1950s was the revived Beardmore, which was introduced after the company no longer had Wolseley Oxfords to sell. Initially, the Mark VII Beardmore used a 1,508cc Ford Consul engine and gearbox, with steering column gearchange, and cross-braced frame upswept over the rear axle. The coachbuilt body had aluminium panelling, and was the work of Windovers Ltd of Hendon, close to the Beardmore works. Windovers were mainly builders of bus and coach bodywork, and before the war they had been among the better-known firms building bodies on high-quality car chassis such as Rolls-Royce and Bentley. The Consul-engined model was launched in 1954 (picture, p143), and was joined in 1958 by a diesel-engined version powered by the Perkins Four 99. This developed 43bhp at 4,000rpm, compared with 59bhp at 4,400rpm from the 1958 Consul Mark II engine but, as with Austins, the oil-engine's greater economy resulted in higher sales. The Mark VII was built in relatively small numbers until the summer of 1967. Beardmore had commissioned a new design, known as the Mark VIII, but their limited share of the market did not justify the necessary re-tooling, and the Mark VIII got no further than a scale model. The design was acquired by Metropolitan Cammell Weymann of Birmingham, whose 1970 Metrocab prototype shows some bodily resemblance to the Beardmore project. Beardmores themselves continued to service their cabs for two years, but in July 1969 they closed down completely. At the end of 1970 there were still 125 Mark VIIs on the London streets.

Austin's second post-war model, the FX4, was announced in September 1958, although a prototype had been operated by York Way Motors since July. It had a completely new body built, like its predecessors, by Carbodies Ltd, and although the wheelbase was the same as that of the FX3, the greater length (four inches) and width (one inch) of the body made the FX4 seem a much larger vehicle. At 31½cwt, it was about 3cwt heavier than the FX3. The rear seat could take three passengers quite comfortably which, with two occasional seats, gave a seating capacity of five. Scotland Yard regulations, however, restricted it to carrying no more than four. The same diesel engine was used as in the FX3, but there were two important mechanical innovations, Borg Warner automatic transmission and coil independent front suspension. Both were being used on a London taxicab for the first time, although the Borg Warner transmission had been installed experimentally on eighteen FX3s operated by York Way Motors, and one of these had covered 70,000 miles by the time the FX4 was introduced. At first, the automatic box was standard equipment but a manual synchromesh box was re-introduced by request later, and in the long run proved more popular, giving better fuel consumption and being cheaper in initial cost. Out of 8,725 FX4s licensed in London in 1970, only 961 had automatic transmission. The FX4 was the first London taxi to have a door to the luggage platform, which meant that the driver no longer needed a partition on his left, and so had more elbow room and better visibility. The near-side front door was adopted on the later Beardmores as well. (Picture, p143.)

Although the FX4 was officially launched at the Commercial Motor Show in September 1958, production was slow to start, and there were only 150 on the road a year later. Deliveries picked up in 1960, and over 13,000 had been sold by Mann & Overton up to October 1971. The FX4 is still in production and shows every sign of remaining London's leading taxicab for many years to come. In its thirteen years of life it has had few changes. Its appearance is almost identical today with that of the 1958 model, though the turn indicator lights have been removed from the sides of the roof to the rear wings, and the tinted glass in the rear window was replaced

Page 125 (above) 1934 Austin TT with Jones single landaulet body, one of the last of the TTs; (below) 1938 Austin LL with Jones single landaulet body

Page 126 (above) 1949 Wolseley Oxford radio cab; *(below)* a 1950
Austin FX3 passing Buckingham Palace

by clear glass in 1969. This was said to make tourists happy and lovers unhappy, the latter doubly so for the new cabs have an interior rear-view mirror in addition to the wing mirrors. Another concession to tourists is the replacement of the illuminated sign, 'For Hire', by the single word 'Taxi', now a completely international word.

The 2.2-litre diesel engine of the FX4 was supplemented by a petrol engine of similar capacity, as used in Austin vans and in the Gipsy cross-country vehicle. This developed 23 per cent more power than the diesel, giving a maximum speed of 75mph. In 1971 the diesel's capacity went up to 2.5 litres. The petrol engine was more silent and caused less vibration than the diesel as well as being cheaper, but its greater running costs kept sales down. Fewer than 10 per cent of the FX4s licensed in 1970 had petrol engines. The diesel, however, was severely criticised by the Noise Abatement Society in 1968, and has been called 'the proprietors' darling and the cabbies' devil'. It is probably true that a slightly higher proportion of owner-drivers use petrol-engined cabs than do fleet operators, but then the owner-driver is more likely to undertake the longer journeys where the higher speed of the petrol-engined cab is important.

Fewer FX4s were exported than their predecessors, because BMC found that export business without adequate spares and service facilities tended to discredit the group's products as a whole. It was uneconomic to maintain spares in foreign cities for a vehicle whose total production was less than 1,500 per year. In 1959, the Yellow Cab Co of Philadelphia put two FX4 diesels on the road experimentally, thus bringing the wheel full circle from the 1920s when Yellow Cabs had run in London. Another attempt was made in the United States in 1968 when a petrol-engined, automatic gearbox FX4 was tried out in New York at the suggestion of Mayor John Lindsay. Worried about transportation problems, he felt that a smaller cab would be a solution to traffic congestion. This

H

experiment was also conducted by Yellow Cab Co, but they were not very impressed; even if delivered in a batch of 1,000, the price could not be lower than $3,500, compared with $2,700 for the larger American sedans already in use. And despite its small engine, the FX4 gave no better mileage than 12 to the gallon. The New York public, on the other hand, was almost unanimously enthusiastic. They praised the easy access and headroom, and one lady remarked 'My small dog loves the expanse of floor'.

If America would not buy new London cabs, a flourishing market grew up for second-hand ones. Their distinctive appearance and excellent manoeuvreability made them attractive as shopping cars, and since 1967 the London General Cab Co has been exporting about 200 cabs per year, initially FX3s but latterly FX4s as well. Most go to North America, but collectors on the continent of Europe have taken some, and they have also been sold to Ghana for another lease of regular cab life. The British Ambassador in Belgrade used an FX3 as his personal transport for a few years. Prices to Americans range from $350 for a cab straight off the street (with Ministry of Transport test certificate) to $1,850 for a completely reconditioned model. The McCulloch Oil Co has bought six which will ply across the rebuilt London Bridge at Lake Havasu, Arizona. In England, a few city businessmen use FX4s suitably modified for private operation, while the taxi-based town broughams of the late Mr Nubar Gulbenkian were among the most distinctive features of London traffic in the 1960s. With custom coachwork by F.L.M. (Panelcraft) Ltd, the second of these cost £3,500 in 1966, and was sold at auction in 1971 for £6,300.

In the spring of 1963 a completely new shape of taxicab appeared in London. This was the Winchester, the first London cab to have a fibreglass body. It was a true owner-driver's taxi; the design having been worked out by a group of men with practical experience of the trade, led by Mr K. E.

Drummond, managing director of Winchester Automobiles (West End) Ltd, a subsidiary of Westminster Motor Insurance, a group formed after the war to specialise in insurance, claims recovery and legal representation for the owner-driver. The Winchester's body was moulded from Cellobond polyester resin reinforced with fibreglass, and had two big advantages, lower weight and freedom from rust, which was the bane of pressed steel cabs. Among refinements was a recessed step to provide easy access and which was automatically lit up when the doors were opened. The original bodies were coloured in two tones of grey, but later ones were black. The engine was a Perkins Four 99, but this was soon replaced by a Ford Cortina petrol unit which was quieter, more lively and still reasonably economical. This chassis was made by Rubery Owen and the bodies by James Whitson. Later bodies, from 1965, were made by Wincanton Transport & Engineering, a subsidiary of the Unigate Dairy Group. The body was completely redesigned in 1968, giving it an appearance closer to that of the Austin cab. Necessary alterations to the chassis were made by Keewest Developments Ltd of Botley, Hants, who are the current builders of Winchester chassis, the bodies still being made by Wincanton Transport & Engineering. At the end of 1970 there were 139 Winchester taxicabs in service in London. (Picture, p144.)

There were no post-war series production London taxicabs other than those described. In 1958, Birch Brothers built an experimental cab using a Standard diesel engine, Standard Ten bonnet and grille, and shooting-brake type body, but it never went into service. In 1970, Metropolitan Cammell Weymann introduced the Metrocab, but this is still experimental at the time of writing, and is described in Chapter Nine.

An important development in the post-war cab trade was the introduction of the radiocab. These had first appeared in England in 1947, at Cambridge and Bournemouth, and the first radio-controlled cabs appeared on the streets of London two years later. Radiocabs (London) Ltd was set up in 1953 by a group of owner-drivers who clubbed together to buy the station and paid £25 each for two-way sets and £1 8s (£1.40) per week for using the service. Radiocabs owned the circuit, and hired out sets (themselves hired from and maintained by the manufacturers) to a dozen firms as well as to their owner-driver members. They had a central transmitter, twenty-six telephonists and sixteen dispatchers working shifts to fill a twenty-four-hour day. However, increasing traffic congestion restricted the value of their service; sometimes a cab might be only a quarter of a mile from the address from which it was ordered and still take half an hour to get there. Admittedly, this was only true in the few square miles of central London, but even a ten-minute delay tended to destroy customer confidence in the service, and after six years Radiocabs gave up. However there were still some 600 radiocabs operated by other firms, and the number has increased to about 800 at the time of writing.

The Licensed Taxi Drivers' Association would like to see all London cabs equipped with radio, for only then do they feel that they could offer a service in every way as good as that of the minicab companies, which have always relied on radio. Apart from normal passenger work, radiocabs have rushed blood plasma and oxygen from one hospital to another, and have helped the police with radio reports of accidents, fires or crime. In the summer of 1966, 350 owner-drivers helped in the search for the killers of three policemen at Shepherds Bush in London.

CHAPTER EIGHT

MICHAEL GOTLA'S PRIVATE ARMY

In 1961 the London cab trade suffered the biggest threat of the century, with the introduction of the so-called 'minicabs'. The question of a smaller taxicab had come up in the House of Commons in November 1960, when Mr Rupert Speir, a Conservative member of parliament, described the current taxi service as inadequate. In particular, he criticised out-of-date design and laws, and called for a city-wide telephone service in which an easily-remembered code such as 'TAX' or 'CAB' could be linked to all taxi ranks. He also called for a smaller cab, and this drew a reply from Mr Dennis Vosper, Minister of State at the Home Office, the main points of which were as follows:

> A minicab type of vehicle might not be able to stand the strain of cab work in London, where the average annual mileage was 40,000.
> Small cabs had been tried before, but there had been little demand, and they had been withdrawn. [He presumably meant the two-seaters, which had never, in fact, been given a chance to test the demand.]
> Limited demand would mean that manufacturers would not be interested in making a small cab.

As far as parliament was concerned, the matter lapsed for the time being, but on 9 December 1960 the first announcement of a minicab service appeared. This came from Michael Gotla, managing director of Welbeck Motors Ltd, a firm which sold and hired out cars. Mr Gotla, who had read law at

University College, London, came to the motor trade by way
of advertising, and began with private-hire chauffeur work in
the evenings. By 1960 he had built Welbeck Motors, which
was financed by Sir Isaac Woolfson's General Guarantee Corporation, into a flourishing business with a staff of a hundred.
His proposal was to put two hundred 'small car taxis' on the
road during 1961. They were to be driven by women as well
as by men, the drivers being guided over the radio when
necessary by three ex-taxi drivers who would advise on the
best routes. The drivers were to wear khaki shirts, trousers
and forage caps, this earning them their nickname of 'Gotla's
Private Army'. As they were not licensed by Scotland Yard
they were forbidden to ply for hire, but Gotla did not want to
rely entirely on telephone bookings. His solution was to tell
prospective passengers to hail the first minicab they saw; the
driver would then hand them the cab's telephone by means
of which they could order another cab from headquarters.
Hopefully, they said that the second cab would be on the spot
'in a moment'. Thus the fare would have 'hired a car', not
'hailed a taxi'. The price was to be 1s (5p) per mile with no
initial charge or extras (the current taxi rate was 1s 9d [9p] for
the first three-fifths of a mile, then 1s 3d [6½p] per mile, plus
extras for luggage and passengers above one). The cars chosen
were to be Renault Dauphines or Ford Prefects.

Although the Welbeck minicabs were the first to be announced, and ultimately the best known, they were beaten
onto the streets by those of two other companies. The first of
these was Carline of Wimbledon, who put a fleet of two-door
Ford Anglias into service in March 1961. They set up ranks
on private sites such as builders' yards and shop drives, and
tried as far as possible to locate these ranks near busy spots
such as greyhound-racing tracks, football grounds and railway
stations. To avoid the charge of plying for hire, they said that
the last cab on the rank would be the headquarters cab. The
fare would give his instructions to the driver of this cab, who

would send him to the leading cab, meanwhile radioing instructions to the leading cab's driver. In Carline's view this
constituted an advance booking, albeit one of only a few
seconds. Carline had twelve cabs in use by mid-March. Their
first trip into central London took place on 7 March when the
Evening News motoring correspondent W. R. Paulson took
one from Wimbledon to his Fleet Street office. The cost was
10s (50p). In addition to ordinary hirings, Carline planned
two services, a credit card for customers who would be sent a
bill at the end of each month, and shared hiring, in which
three people would be taken from Wimbledon to the City
and back for 35s (£1.75). They had a large number of appli-
cations from potential drivers, but many were weeded out by
the geography and driving tests which the company conducted. Details of the former were not given to the press, but it
must have been much less demanding than 'the Knowledge'
expected of all taxi drivers by Scotland Yard, for this often
takes eighteen months for a driver to learn, whereas Carline
men were in action within a month of the scheme's announcement. Carline did, however, insist on ten years' driving experience and an Advanced Motorists Licence. The latter is
not required of taxi-drivers by Scotland Yard, and many
London drivers would question its value in the metropolis.

The second minicab company to get on the road was Sylvester Car Hire, operating from Dolphin Square, Pimlico.
They used the Fiat Multipla, an ingenious little vehicle based
on the Fiat 600 car but with the driver seated beside the
engine, and accommodation for four passengers behind him.
The Sylvester cabs were the only minicabs to have meters.
Rates were 1s 6d (7½p) for the first mile, and 1s (5p) per mile
thereafter.

By March 1961 both the popular press and the cab trade
were very much aware of the new cabs. The press was generally in favour of the new project, calling it 'the first notable
innovation in taxi services since horse cabs were replaced'.

Minicabs obtained all the sympathy traditionally accorded to the newcomer and the 'little man' fighting against what the journalists like to call the monopoly of the cab trade. The very size of the minicabs tended to reinforce the 'little man' image, but this was rather deceptive, for Welbeck Motors became the largest fleet owner in Europe, while many of the maligned taxicabs were owner-driven. However, the press generally reserved their criticism for the taxi system, agreeing that the individual driver was a good fellow. An exception was *The New Daily*, itself trying to break a big monopoly and almost obsessively concerned with the interests of the public against organisations of all kinds. This newspaper alleged that taxi drivers were arrogant, rude and unhelpful. One of the staunchest supporters of the taxi drivers was the *Daily Worker*, which carried a number of articles by drivers setting out their case against the minicab.

The licensed taxi driver has many legitimate complaints against minicabs, but they can be grouped under two headings, the driver, and his vehicle. Ever since 1907 a taxi driver has had to undergo the strict tests of knowledge, driving, health and character, described in Chapter Four, whereas though some minicab companies may have insisted on tests of a kind, there was no minimum requirement save a current ordinary driving licence. As Maurice Levinson pointed out in his book *Taxi*, 'If a taxi-driver is mad enough to rape one of his passengers and loses his licence, there is nothing to stop him driving a minicab and raping another'. The same situation applies to the cabs themselves. A taxi has to conform to a very strict specification on design and construction (see Appendix 3) which is the main reason for its high cost, and also has to undergo an annual inspection. The irony is that a cab which has failed this inspection can go onto the streets the next day as a minicab! Although the gaudy, eye-catching minicabs lasted barely a year, the breed did not disappear; the threat to the legitimate cab trade still exists, and is the more insidious as the minicabs are now operated by countless small companies and are indistinguishable from private cars.

The initial reaction of the cab trade to the minicabs was strikingly similar to their attitude to the two-seaters, being a mixture of 'They won't get far', and 'They must be stopped'. Soon, however, it was realised that the minicabs would not be stopped unless something drastic was done about them. On 8 March 1961 about 3,000 taxi drivers held an evening meeting at the Seymour Hall, Marylebone. Mr Jim Francis, general secretary of the cab drivers' section of the Transport & General Workers' Union, said that Mr R. A. Butler, the Home Secretary, had a few more days to sort out the problem, after which taxi drivers would have to consider what steps to take to protect their interests. The drivers passed a resolution to the effect that they were profoundly disturbed by the threat to their living standards, and set up a fighting fund of 1d per week per member. A number of them, led by Jim Francis, formed the London Cab Trade Crisis Committee. On 15 March the Home Secretary was asked in the House of Commons to make the proposed Welbeck method of hiring minicabs illegal. He replied that if the police thought that this constituted plying for hire within the meaning of the Metropolitan Public Carriage Act of 1869, prosecutions might follow. This vague, equivocal statement did not worry the minicab operators at all, and curiously, the Motor Cab Owner Drivers' Association was pleased, adding that if nothing was being done about it, they themselves would gather evidence and start prosecutions.

Meanwhile, Welbeck Motors had chosen Renault Dauphines for their fleet, and had placed a £560,000 order for 800 cars, the largest single order ever placed by a British buyer with a continental manufacturer. The original colour was to be yellow, but red was later chosen as this was a regular Dauphine colour and therefore cheaper. One factor in the choice of Renault was that the French company did not seek to bind Welbeck to the exclusive use of their cars. The first Sylvester cabs went into service on 17 March, and the company claimed to have been rushed off their feet within a few days. The first incident occurred when two taxi drivers 'boxed in' a Sylvester cab and complained to a policeman that it was plying for hire. The driver said that he was looking for the address of a fare who had telephoned a booking. A few days later a minicab was hemmed in by thirty taxis in Belgrave Square, and had to radio to headquarters for help. The taxi drivers were booked by the police for obstruction.

Meanwhile Carline were operating a *free* service, with tipping banned, from London Airport and mainline railway stations back to their depot at Wimbledon. The reason for this was that even though they had been legitimately hired to take a fare to airport or station, by law they were forbidden to pick up a casual fare for the return journey as this would constitute plying for hire. If no payment was involved, however, the major element of plying for hire was removed; they had to return to Wimbledon anyway, and might as well pick up some goodwill and a possible future client in the process. The cabbies, however, were soon wise to this, and on 6 June a girl driver, 25-year-old Valerie Atkins, was hemmed in at Waterloo station and had to phone to headquarters for help. The police moved her on. By this time there had been dozens of incidents against minicabs, especially false telephone calls, but also some cases of hemming in, splashing with paint and overturning. Mr R. W. Heath, managing director of Carline, employed private detectives to watch likely trouble spots. Jim Francis of the Transport & General Workers' Union said that his men had been instructed not to molest the minicab drivers, but feeling was so high that he could offer no guarantee against some incidents. The minicab drivers said that about 10 per cent of cab drivers were making things difficult for them, especially the older men.

The government was still disinclined to become involved

with the situation. On 7 June Dennis Vosper said in the Commons; 'To the extent that the entry into this field of additional firms operating smaller vehicles at a relatively low tariff will enable these facilities to be enjoyed by a wider section of the community, the development is in keeping with post-war trends in our society, and fully accords with the policy of the present administration'. This was gleefully quoted by Welbeck Motors in one of several full-page advertisements which they ran in the *Evening Standard* during early June. A typical one ran, 'Wish us luck...don't listen to the twaddle talk turned out by the London taxi trade. We say for the umpteenth time: we are not in competition with the traditional London taxi: we are creating a new market'.

On Monday, 19 June, the first Welbeck minicab was released onto the road by Monsieur Guitton of the French Ministry of Industry and Commerce. He emptied a bottle of champagne over the bonnet of one of the red Dauphines, which had been hoisted onto the roof of Welbeck's premises in Taunton Street; the cab was then lowered to the street and set off in search of its first fare. That day's *Evening News* had a big feature on Welbeck Motors, including an advertisement in the following coy vein: 'Every day from now on, five little Welbeck Minicabs will be born, and by Christmas calling for a Welbeck Minicab will be as natural—and as certain—as turning on a tap.'

The original Welbeck cabs were plastered with advertisements, among the most familiar being those for Air France, Pakamac plastic raincoats, Tizer soft drinks and Cyril Lord carpets. Each cab's advertising space was rented out to a bulk advertiser; the return to Welbeck was £75 per cab per annum, and this income was essential to the profitable running of the enterprise. When advertisements began to fall off, Welbeck ran into serious difficulties. The fleet consisted of 250 cabs straightaway, with 500 more promised over the following two months. Michael Gotla announced that he would ask for some form of government control of all cabs in six months' time, if his scheme was successful. He added that he would be quite happy to let the traditional cabs control central London if he could look after the suburbs. This statement, however, was not reflected in any absence of minicabs from central London.

There were few awkward incidents on the first day; one taxi driver who was involved in a *bona fide* accident with a Welbeck minicab drove to the headquarters to explain and apologise. But within a week, there were quite a number of unpleasant incidents, including minicab passengers being hauled out of cabs and insulted, and in one case assaulted. By October the 'minicab war' could be justifiably so described, with drivers of both factions being assaulted by their rivals. Some of the incidents reported included squirting instant solder into door and ignition locks, knocking holes in body-work, slashing seats and pouring foul-smelling liquids into the cars' interiors. As Welbeck and other minicab firms relied so much on the telephone they were naturally vulnerable to the wave of false calls made by taxi drivers' wives and girl friends. One advertisement appeared in a local paper reading 'Attractive three-room flat to let in good district. Only £3 10s per week. Ring WELbeck 4440.' The Welbeck Motors switchboard was inundated with callers! This was particularly serious for Welbeck, as one of the chief customer complaints against minicabs was slow answering of the switchboard.

A racial element also came into the dispute when taxi drivers, many of whom are Jewish, claimed that Welbeck Motors refused to employ Jews, and that one of the Welbeck drivers was a notorious fascist. At about this time there was an unpleasant and well-publicised incident between a Jewish taxi driver and Mrs Colin Jordan, the wife of the British fascist leader. This was quite unconnected with Welbeck Motors, but the link between racism and minicabs had been established in the public's mind. This adverse publicity had two effects on Welbeck's finances; in September, Air France withdrew their advertising on the grounds that it was unseemly for a foreign firm to be mixed up in a British dispute, and in November Isaac Woolfson's General Guarantee Corporation withdrew its support and sold its shares to the chairman, Mr R. S. Walker. Shortly after this, Michael Gotla resigned and started up a completely new car sales business in Worthing.

The Air France withdrawal was followed by similar action from most other advertisers, and this was the major cause of Welbeck's subsequent financial difficulties. Advertising revenue was equal to at least $1\frac{1}{2}$d per passenger mile, and the only way to compensate for its loss was to raise fares. This Welbeck did, to 1s 4d (7p) per mile and then to 1s 8d ($8\frac{1}{2}$p) per mile, which made their rates higher than those of taxis for longer journeys. Another problem for Welbeck was a very rapid turnover in drivers. At one time Gotla said that they had been hiring 100 drivers a week and firing 60 to 65 of them. Some were not efficient enough to earn a reasonable 'take', while others earned their £8 per week minimum wage in three days and spent the rest of the week sunning themselves in the park. Yet others were careless of their cars' condition and appearance, or earned the firm a bad name by indulging in some of the violent tactics mentioned earlier. Clearly the free-wheeling 'anti-Establishment' nature of minicab work was likely to attract a proportion of unsuitable men, some verging on the criminal—a problem that is still with the minicab business.

There were few police prosecutions of minicabs for illegal plying for hire, but cabbies initiated their own private prosecutions with some success. The first of these was brought by Edward Wall on 16 July against a Welbeck driver and Welbeck Motors. In this case the driver had not received radio instructions but verbal instructions from another driver just around the corner. The driver was fined £5, and Welbeck the same amount plus £26 5s costs. A number of similar prosecutions followed, but in November there came an incident which caused a great deal of ill-feeling. Two cabbies were jailed for three months and banned from driving for three years for hemming in a minicab on Brompton Road at three o'clock one morning. This followed a sentence of two months' jail and twelve months' driving ban on another cabby a week earlier. After an emergency meeting, the London Cab Trade Crisis Committee called a forty-eight hour strike, which was observed by about 1,000 drivers.

The fact that illegal plying by minicabs had been largely ignored by the police, who then came down hard on licensed cab-drivers for obstruction, did nothing to improve relations between the drivers and the police, which had been difficult ever since the nineteenth century. Matters became even worse when it was revealed that some policemen had been driving minicabs in their spare time, although these were only a small minority and were severely censured by their superiors for working in off-duty hours. In June 1962 the prison sentences on the two cab drivers were quashed on appeal, being replaced by fines of £100, and the driving bans were also lifted.

Between Spring 1961 and Spring 1962 no fewer than twenty-nine minicabs firms sprang up in London, but the original companies which had attracted so much attention were by now all in difficulties. In December 1961 Sylvester Car Hire changed their name to Metrocabs and their function to a cheap hire service at rates of 1s 6d to 1s 8d per mile, depending on the size of car. Carline were given notice to quit their premises by Wimbledon Council and the company was put up for sale, while Welbeck were forced to remove all their advertising after a High Court ruling by the Lord Chief Justice, Lord Parker. This arose from a prosecution brought by a taxi driver, Emmanuel Rose, against Welbeck Motors in November 1961, when he saw a Welbeck cab apparently plying for hire in East London. He reported this to a policeman, who ordered the minicab to move on, but later it returned, and the two drivers went to the police station together. The magistrate's court dismissed the case on the grounds that there was no evidence of solicitation and that the driver could simply have been awaiting instructions by radio. Mr Rose's appeal against the decision was heard by Lord Parker on 31 May 1962, and in his ruling the following day he held that the very presence of the company's name and telephone number on its minicabs was, in effect, saying 'I am a cab of Welbeck Motors and I am for hire'. Within hours of the ruling being announced Welbeck Motors flashed a message to all their 300 cabs, 'Drive to a side street and take off your ads—quickly!' The commercial advertisements had already disappeared, and with the removal of the name and telephone number Welbeck cabs became indistinguishable from any privately-owned Renault Dauphines. Some firms subsequently painted their minicabs in vivid colours such as red, white and blue squares and diamonds, but this fashion did not last for long.

By January 1963, there were only 200 minicabs in London, compared with the 5,000 that had been promised eighteen months earlier. The first phase of the minicab invasion was over, and as far as the press was concerned the drama had gone out of the subject for good. There were, however, two humorous attempts to provide a cheaper taxi service which attracted some attention. In March 1963 that tireless supporter of small cabs, Mr Rupert Speir, MP, suggested a two-seater three-wheeled rickshaw based on the Vespa motor-scooter, and was photographed riding to the House of Commons in one. A *Daily Express* reporter also tried out a rickshaw and found it more manoeuvreable than a conventional taxi and more fun as a novelty, but it gave him a cold ride, even in April. 'Rickshaw taxis need rickshaw weather to go with them,' he said.

Even more draughty was the moped taxi service proposed in 1964 as a method of beating traffic jams. The mopeds charged 2s (10p) for a 1¼ mile ride, and were driven by girls. 'Even a little rain might be bearable with your arms clasped around a slim waist' said *The Guardian*, adding that passengers who wanted a crash helmet would be provided with one. This service operated for only a few days.

By 1966 minicabs had sprung up in increasing numbers again, some operated by reputable companies and others by fly-by-night concerns with incompetent or even ex-criminal drivers whose cars were not properly insured, leaving passengers without redress if injured. A frequent complaint was that drivers did not know their way around London. Apart from the direct threat to their livelihood, the taxi drivers were particularly incensed by the way the incompetence and bad behaviour of minicab drivers so often rubbed off on them. For example, when a minicab driver snatched a company director's astrakhan hat because he thought his tip was insufficient, the papers carried the headline 'London cabby steals hat'. Many of the complaints about extortionate fares from London Airport relate to minicab men, as do those of taking foreign girls to abortion clinics.

A minicab bureau was set up at Victoria Coach Station in the summer of 1966 but was closed after pressure by the Transport & General Workers' Union. As the coach drivers were also union members, the T.G.W.U. were in a strong position to force the closure. They did not call a strike, but recommended a 'co-ordinated rest day' in which all London taxi drivers, whether union members or not, took their day off at the same time. This took place on 14 June 1966, when the only taxis to be seen were those carrying union members to meetings. There were one or two violent incidents, as at Waterloo when a minicab driver panicked, grazed the leg of one picketing taxi driver and carried another spreadeagled on his bonnet for fifty yards. The public suffered some inconvenience, but motorists had an easy day, and Scotland Yard reported that the evening rush-hour traffic jams were far less prolonged than usual.

Page 143 (above) 1954 Beardmore Mark VII; (below) 1969 Austin
FX4

Page 144
(top)
1963 Winchester
Mark I;

(middle)
1970 Winchester
Mark II;

(bottom)
second prototype
of 1971 Metrocab,
photographed
before going into
service with the
London General
Cab Co

In April 1966 a National Minicab Association was started, with the idea of bringing together all the reputable companies and keeping the fly-by-nights out. The association's president, Mr Frank Smith, wanted legislation to ensure registration of minicab drivers, who would have to carry identity cards similar to the taxi drivers' green or yellow badges, and regular inspection of cars. This has been proposed more recently in the Maxwell Stamp Report (see Chapter Nine), but it is too early yet to say how it will be implemented. The National Minicab Association never attracted more than ten companies into membership, and after a year only seven remained. It seemed that the minicab business was content to remain unorganised and operators were not particularly interested in improving their image so long as they could make quick profits. In March 1967, 5,000 taxi drivers lobbied parliament to protest against minicabs being allowed to carry passengers without adequate insurance or supervision. The protest was called because the then Home Secretary, Mr Roy Jenkins, had promised to meet a small deputation, but had cancelled the meeting at the last minute as he was speaking in the House.

In May 1967 a new union for taxi drivers was formed, the Licensed Taxi Drivers' Association. Their initial aim was to provide every licensed cab with two-way radio, and thus give an unrivalled service which would mean the end of the minicabs. However, the L.T.D.A. has since become the leading union in giving vigorous support to taxi drivers in every kind of dispute, and many drivers feel that it protects their interests far more effectively than the T.G.W.U. Under its chairman, Mr William D'Arcy, the L.T.D.A. has been in the forefront of protests against the use of minicabs by hotels and hospitals, and has opposed the licensing of minicabs, as suggested in the Maxwell Stamp Report. At the initial meeting in the Festival Hall, London, the L.T.D.A. enrolled over 1,100 members, and by May 1971 their numbers had risen to 4,500. The association publishes a fortnightly magazine, *Taxi*, edited by

J

the taxi driver author Maurice Levinson.

Legally speaking, the minicab disappeared from London on 15 July 1968, the day on which the London Cab Act 1968 came into force. One of the provisions of the Act was to make illegal the words 'taxi' or 'cab', whether they were used on the vehicles or in any form of advertising, unless they referred to licensed taxicabs. In theory, this even applied to vehicles coming into London from outside with a fare, but it was pointed out that a taxi driver from, say, Brighton, could hardly cover up his 'taxi' sign with sticky paper when he entered the Metropolitan area. If, however, having deposited his fare at a London address, he took up another fare, even from the same address, he would be liable to prosecution.

The first firm to be prosecuted under the new Act was Dial-a-Cab (Minicabs) Ltd, which issued an advertisement including the word 'cab'. They were fined £10 in February 1969. The second prosecution came in March of the same year, when a Lewisham firm was fined £16 with 20 guineas costs because their cars carried telephone number signs. The maximum fine is £20 for a first offence, and £50 for a second. As a result of this legislation, the word 'minicab' has almost entirely disappeared from advertising, but a look at a 1971 London Telephone Directory showed no fewer than thirty-three companies using 'minicab' as part of their name.

CHAPTER NINE

TAXICABS TODAY AND TOMORROW

The Austin FX4 is now over thirteen years old, and its appearance has undergone almost no change since it was introduced. Many people both in and outside the cab trade have wondered for how much longer the design will soldier on, and have put forward various suggestions for a replacement. In August 1968 the Consumer Council suggested a smaller cab, pointing out that at the moment a single passenger in a taxi took up forty square feet of road space compared with the six square feet of a bus passenger in a fully loaded bus. The Council called for a more compact cab, but preserving the ease of entry, good lock and sturdiness of the present cab. They thought that the latter should be retained for some work, but recognised that the problems of operating two types of cab side by side might be considerable. The trend would be for one type to drive the other off the road (how reminiscent of 1926!). The Council also suggested a passenger-sharing system with 'taxi wardens' at big stations to organise parties of those who wished to go in the same direction.

In 1970, a student of industrial design at the Central School of Art and Design, 24-year-old John Redmond, produced a design for a six-passenger taxi-cum-minibus with an overall length of thirteen feet. During normal hours it would operate as an ordinary taxi, but in the morning and evening rush hours it would be a variable direction minibus. The first passenger to hail it would set the destination, which would then be indicated on a panel above the windscreen, and other passengers going in that direction could hail the vehicle if they wished. The taxi was to be powered by two electric motors fed by lithium-nickel fluoride batteries with eight hours' running time. A mock-up model was built as part of Mr Redmond's project.

A more conventional and less futuristic proposal for a new taxi came from the staff of *Autocar* magazine in June 1971. They based their design on the Bedford CF van chassis which is powered by a Vauxhall Victor 2000 engine under a short bonnet. The combination of a short bonnet and a van-type body meant that interior accommodation for four passengers could be combined with an overall length of only 12ft 6in, compared with 15ft for the FX4. The *Autocar* design complied with Scotland Yard regulations in every way, and yet had a distinctive, functional appearance which broke away from that of the conventional taxi. However, when Vauxhall Motors were asked if they would be interested in building such a vehicle, they replied that the number of taxis they could sell would not justify the amount of development work and retooling involved.

This, of course, is always the biggest snag in any plans for a new design of taxi, and is the reason why Londoners are likely to be using mainly FX4s for a long time to come. Even in private-car design, where the volume of production may run into hundreds of thousands, the ever-increasing cost and the labour problems involved in even a minor design change are slowing down the rate of alteration. The London cab trade is unlikely to absorb more than 1,500 taxis per year and, on the whole, provincial operators prefer to use ordinary saloon cars. So, despite the cabbies' grumbles about the poor performance, noise and bulk of their cabs (the public are on the whole more satisfied with the existing machines than are the drivers),

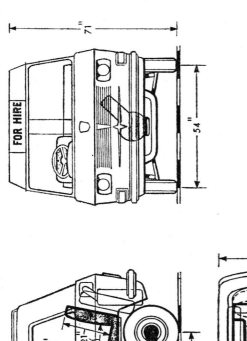

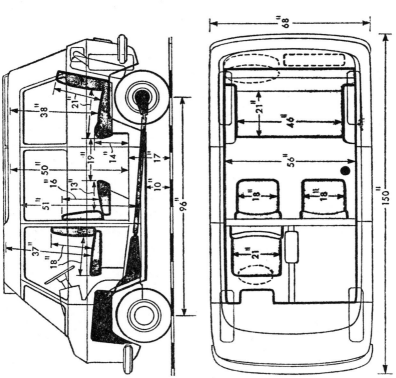

FOR HIRE

71"

54"

The Autocar's design for a
taxi based on the Bedford
CF van chassis

38" 21"
50" 19" 14"
51" 16" 13" 17"
37" 18" 10"
18"

96"

68"
21"
46"
56"
18" 18"
21"
150"

J*

there is unlikely to be a revolutionary new cab in the near future. Nevertheless, an improved FX4 was shown at the 1971 London Motor Show, with a 2.52-litre diesel engine to replace the old 2.2-litre unit. The new engine is more powerful and quieter, and complies with forthcoming regulations on smoke emission and noise. The rear axle ratio is now higher and this increases the safe cruising speed, an important factor for cabs making use of the motorway to London Airport.

FX4 prices (October 1971) range from £1,487 for a 2.2-litre petrol-engined cab, through £1,612 for the diesel synchromesh model, to £1,689 for the diesel with automatic gearbox. These prices do not include the meter, which is, in fact, rented for a quarterly payment ranging from £5.70 to £6.00 according to the make. A number of extras are available, including rim-bellishers, electric clock and fog lamps, but the most expensive special order is for an alternative colour to the traditional black. This must be a colour from the current Austin chart, and costs £25. A number of owner-drivers have ordered cabs in blue, red, or silver, but they represent a very small proportion of the cabs on the road. Probably the ultimate in FX4s was offered recently by Bristol Street Motors Ltd. This was a petrol-engined cab with forward-facing occasional seats, heavy carpeting and lambswool rug, soundproofing to roof and body, radio and twin speakers in passenger compartment, electric windows in each door, twin cigar-lighters and ashtrays in the rear compartment, and a fully carpeted boot. It was finished in special dark blue paintwork and cost £2,600.

Apart from the design studies already mentioned, one new project has actually reached the road. This is the Metrocab, two prototypes of which have been built by Metropolitan-Cammell-Weymann Ltd of Birmingham, well-known as builders of bus and coach bodies and underground railway carriages. The Metrocab is powered by a 52bhp 1,760cc Perkins diesel engine, and uses a gearbox and transmission from the Ford Transit van, a Ford Cortina radiator grille, and has a fibreglass body. This is lighter than either the Winchester or Austin bodies, and has the greatest window area of any London taxi yet built. The Metrocab re-introduces the running board for easier entry, although the concealed step behind the door, as used on the Winchester, is probably the better method of easing entry and certainly the better looking. The first prototype Metrocab went into service with the London General Cab Co in June 1970, and the second prototype, slightly modified, in December 1971. At the time of writing, no decision has been made on whether the Metrocab will be produced in quantity. (Picture, p144.)

The relative popularity of different taxicabs is given in the following table:

Cabs licensed during 1970

Austin FX4D (automatic gearbox)	961
Austin FX4D (synchromesh gearbox)	7,124
Austin FX4 (petrol)	640
Beardmore	125
Winchester	139
Metrocab	1
Total	8,990

New cabs licensed during 1970

Austin FX4D (automatic gearbox)	230
Austin FX4D (synchromesh gearbox)	1,168
Austin FX4 (petrol)	80
Winchester	33
Metrocab	1
Total	1,512

A new fuel recently introduced to the cab trade is liquid propane gas. In April 1970 W. H. Cook & Co of Hammersmith, London, put three propane-converted FX4s on the road. The conversion was done by the Lipton Liquid Propane Carburetter Co, an offshoot of L. Lipton & Co, manufacturers of fork-lift trucks, who turned to propane during the Suez fuel crisis of 1956. The conversion involves fitting a gas cylinder in the boot, a regulator to reduce the gas to atmospheric pressure, and an adaptor to the carburetter. About 100lb is added to the weight of the cab, and the cost of conversion is £150, but there is a considerable saving in fuel costs. Propane costs 16p per gallon, compared with 32p for petrol, and 30p for DERV (Diesel Engine Road Vehicle) fuel, and W. H. Cook estimate that the cost of conversion is covered in seven to eight months of running. This is largely due to the fact that liquid propane is not taxed as a vehicle fuel at the moment. If its use ever becomes really widespread, doubtless a tax will be placed upon it. Other advantages of propane are that there are no fumes from the exhaust, the engine is quieter, and wear and tear on moving parts of the engine are much less. By March 1972, Cooks had converted nearly 200 cabs to propane.

The greatest point of friction between cabbies and public during the 1960s was the price of the run to, or from, London Airport. Up to 1968, the normal rates applied for a journey of up to six miles, but for that portion of the journey beyond six miles the rate was negotiable between the driver and his passenger. The amount varied greatly; the cabbies quoted £2.50 to £2.75 as an average charge, while a newspaper survey of thirteen journeys from the West End to the airport made in 1965 revealed the following charges: one driver charged £2.25; three charged £2.75; three charged £2.50; five charged £3.00; and one charged £3.50.

The return journey always seemed to cost more, anything up to £4.00 being asked, while there were isolated cases of £6.00 and £7.00. The public made frequent complaints about excessive charges and also about drivers at the airport refusing a short journey to a nearby suburb. The taxi drivers, in turn, complained about the private-hire touts who hung about the arrivals building in plain clothes and 'stole' fares before they could even reach the taxis. The taxi drivers, controlled by airport bye-laws, were not allowed to enter the building and tout for fares. In May 1966 they went on strike in protest against unlicensed touts in the building, and again in May 1968, when a taxi driver was arrested for remaining at the airport after being asked to leave by a policeman. Both these strikes were of less than one day's duration. One private-hire man claimed that he had been threatened with petrol-bombing at his home if he continued to use the airport, but such violence, or even threats of it, were quite untypical. As in the minicab dispute, a few hot-headed men earned the whole trade an undeservedly bad name.

In November 1965 it was announced that the negotiable fare above six miles was to be abolished, but the London Cab Bill putting this into effect was not introduced into parliament until November 1967, and did not come into force until July 1968. The section of the Bill dealing with fares said that the rate beyond six miles was to be double the normal rate. At the prevailing 1968 prices, this meant about £2 5s (£2.25) for the London Airport run, compared with the £2 10s (£2.50) to £2 15s (£2.75) which was normal, and which had been agreed between the British Airports Authority and the Transport & General Workers' Union. To make matters worse, the Owner Drivers' Radio Taxi Service said that some hotel porters exacted ten shillings or a pound from drivers for providing a fare to London Airport, and if the money was not forthcoming they threatened to call in a private-hire car or a minicab next time. A number of drivers threatened to boycott London Airport when the new rules came in, but most drivers gave it a try, and there were no fewer cabs than usual at the airport on the first day of the new fare structure. The private-hire touts remained a threat to the livelihood of taxi drivers at the airport, but their number was greatly reduced in the late summer of 1970 when the hijacking scare brought an unprecedented number of policemen to the airport. By May 1971 most of the extra policemen had left, so the touts returned. The L.T.D.A. again threatened a boycott of the airport if they were not removed, and also a boycott of the

Cromwell Road Air Terminal unless the abortion touts were removed. By mid-June, most of the touts had left both places, so the L.T.D.A. threat was lifted.

The conflict with hotel porters continued, however, and flared up again in August 1971 with the accusation that doormen had taken bribes from minicab firms to choose them in preference to licensed taxis. One minicab firm was alleged to have given a champagne party for head porters of the leading hotels and to have promised each one £50 in return for an undertaking to call that company whenever a guest wanted a cab for a long journey. A boycott of the offending hotels was being planned when the cab section of the T.G.W.U. managed to obtain from a large number of leading hotels a promise that any complaint by a taxi driver of work being taken from him by private-hire drivers would be looked into immediately. Before this promise was obtained, there was a three-day L.T.D.A.-organised boycott of two London hotels, the Clifton-Ford and the Churchill.

It is no easier to forecast the future of the London cab trade today than it would have been at any time in the past, but an idea of possible trends can be gained from the Maxwell Stamp Report of October 1970, to which earlier reference has been made. This report was the result of a three-year enquiry by a committee presided over by merchant banker Arthur Maxwell Stamp. (By a curious coincidence, the chairman of the first enquiry into the London cab trade in 1688 was Sir Thomas Stamp.) They heard evidence from every section of the trade, and also from the public who were asked why they took taxis, whether they preferred taxis to hire cars, and what improvements were needed. The committee found that London had 22,000 private-hire drivers working for firms which ranged from old-established limousine hire companies of the highest reputation down to small fly-by-night concerns whose premises were a small room, one desk and a telephone. These latter acted as agents for a number of owner-driven minicars, and were not really hire companies at all. There was a considerable amount of public concern about the safety of private-hire cars, about the insurance question, and also about the trustworthiness and competence of the drivers. The Commissioner of Metropolitan Police confirmed that a significant number of private-hire drivers had criminal records. About the licensed cab drivers the committee found much less criticism, the main public concern being the vexed question of fares to and from London Airport, the 1968 Act regulating these fares not then having come into force. The design of the taxicab also came in for criticism, the main targets being poor engine performance, braking and vision, and cramped driving space. 'The taxi is in fact much closer to a lorry than a private car . . . the discomfort which the driver has to put up with is intolerable.'

The chief recommendation of the Maxwell Stamp Committee was that all taxis and hire-cars should come under a new independent authority set up by the Greater London Council, but not directly part of the Council. This followed a suggestion made by the G.L.C. in 1968 that, having gained control of London's buses and underground railways, an extension of their control to the cab trade would be a logical step. Taxi drivers were not in favour of the Maxwell Stamp proposals, largely because, of the five or eight members of the proposed new board, not one was to represent the cab trade. One member of this board was to represent consumer interests (which the Consumer Council thought inadequate), and it seems invidious indeed that the trade which provided both machinery and personnel should not have been given at least the same representation as the taxi user. This preoccupation with the interests of 'the public', however, has been characteristic of cab-trade history, as was seen in the two-seater enquiry of 1926 in which 'any questions of hardship' were to take second place to 'the convenience of the public'.

The proposed new authority, to be called the London Taxi

and Hire Car Board, was to be financed by the following licence fees:

Taxicab licence: £21 per annum
Taxi drivers' licence: £10 initially, and £5 on renewal every
     three years
Hire car licence: £3 per annum
Hire car drivers' licence: as for taxi drivers
Hire car operators' licence: £21, renewable every three years

The discrepancy between the cost of a taxi licence and a hire-car licence was explained by the expense involved in the more stringent tests for cabs. There was also to be a charge of £2.50 per annum to drivers for the use of rank telephones, a levy described by the Transport & General Workers' Union as 'impertinent'. In general, however, the union accepted 80 per cent of the report, but rejected the balance, especially the tax on plates and licences. The L.T.D.A. was much less satisfied, criticising in particular the integration of taxi and private-hire operations under one authority, with no relaxations of the strict rules for the former, and little restriction on the freedom of the latter. For example, though taxi fares were to be regulated as before, the committee did not recommend the fixing of private-hire car fares as it would 'stifle competition'. Mr William D'Arcy of the L.T.D.A. pointed out that if hire-car work was seen to be more profitable over a long period, a large number of taxi drivers would go over to hire cars and the taxi population would drop sharply. Already one of the two big radio cab groups, the Owner Drivers' Radio Taxi Service, has begun to use cars to supplement taxis. One recommendation which did please the L.T.D.A. was that there should be a central radio control point which would link up all ranks and from which calls from any part of London could immediately be put through to the nearest rank with an available taxi. This idea, which was very similar to Mr Rupert Speir's suggestion of 'TAX' or 'CAB' telephone codes made in 1960, was described by the L.T.D.A. as the only ray of sunshine to be found in the report.

Just how many of the Maxwell Stamp Committee's recommendations will be put into effect remains to be seen, but it is to be hoped that conditions for the cab trade will not be allowed to deteriorate in favour of private hire, and, indeed, that they will improve. The traditional taxi is not only a cherished part of the London scene, along with double-decker buses and the Changing of the Guard, but an extremely practical vehicle for the traveller, as anyone who has had to cope with cramped, low-slung saloon-car taxis in other cities will testify. However, in a democracy, no one can be compelled to provide a convenient service to the public, and in the long run Londoners will get such service as they are prepared to pay for and as their elected representatives, whether in Parliament or on the Greater London Council, are wise enough to provide.

APPENDICES

APPENDIX 1 : General Rules for Hackney Coaches, 1805

Distance

	s	d
For one mile	1	0
For every half-mile further	0	6

*N.B.: Forty poles or perches make one furlong,
and eight furlongs make one mile.*

Time

	s	d
For forty minutes	1	0
For every twenty minutes after	0	6
For a day (not to exceed twelve hours), and before twelve o'clock at night, and not to exceed twenty miles	18	0

ABSTRACTS of the Acts of Parliament relating to Hackney Coaches

There are 1100 hackney coaches, every proprietor of which pays ten shillings per week.

Every hackney coachman applying for hire within London or Westminster, or the suburbs thereof, shall be obliged, on every day of the week (unless he shall have been out twelve hours, or have other excuse), to go to any place within ten miles, in case he shall have time to return by sun-set, *or the fare shall undertake to return in such coach.* And at any hour of the night, unless he should have been out twelve hours, or have such excuse), to go upon all public turnpike roads, that shall be lighted up, anywhere within the distance of two miles and an half from the ends or extreme parts of the several carriage-way pavements of the cities of London and Westminster, or the suburbs thereof, where a regular continuation of carriage-way pavement doth extend. (32 Geo. 3. c. 47.)

All the space betwixt the stand and the taking up of the fare is to be reckoned into the fare, and the coachman at liberty to take either for the length of ground or time, but not for both. *Ibid.*

NIGHT FARES

Every coach hired between twelve o'clock at night and six in the morning, is entitled to demand sixpence on every shilling in addition to the established rates; no fraction less than sixpence, either for ground or time, to be reckoned; but any coach taken between the hours of ten and twelve at night, is not entitled to the said half fare, even if not discharged till after twelve, except the fare shall exceed two shillings.

COACHES TAKEN OUT OF TOWN

Every coach driven into the country, and discharged at such period of time as will prevent its return before sun-set to the nearest stones end, or to the out-stand, from which it may have been taken, at the rate of five miles in the hour, in such case to be allowed sixpence per mile for such ground he may have to return before sunset, and full fare for such remaining ground as remains after sunset, computing the full fare into one ground or distance, as if the fare returned in the coach; but if the sun is set at the time of discharge, in such case, full fare for the whole ground.

When the average price of oats, computed according to 31 Geo. 3 c. 30 shall exceed 25s per quarter, the commissioners may cause an addition to be made to the fares, viz:

Upon every fare amounting to two shillings, the additional sum of sixpence.

Upon every fare amounting to four shillings, the additional sum of one shilling.

And so upon every increase of two shillings the additional sum of sixpence.

But such additional fare is not to be payable unless the coach be taken the full distance, or kept in waiting the full period, for which the original fare is allowed, and the commissioners are to publish notice of the increase in the *Gazette*; which increase may be continued till thirty days after the average price of oats shall be reduced to one guinea per quarter. (the above increase of fares commenced December 21, 1804, by order of the commissioners; and which increase is added to the whole of the fares in this work.) But when the average price of oats are reduced to one guinea per quarter, the following deductions must be made on all the fares: above two shillings, and under five shillings, sixpence; five shillings, and under seven shillings and sixpence, one shilling; seven shillings and sixpence, and under ten shillings, one shilling and sixpence; ten shillings and upwards, two shillings. (Of which reduction the commissioners are to give notice in the *London Gazette*.)

All coachmen who ply for hire at the theatres, or other places of public resort, or who shall place their coaches at the side of the street, or in any situation where they do not usually ply, shall be considered liable to be hired and taken, as if on a stand. And on complaint being made to the commissioners will be fined for refusal, unless such coachman shall produce positive proof of being actually hired at the time; and if such proof shall be really brought forward, in such case the commissioners have power to award to such coachman a reasonable compensation for loss of time on being summoned.

If any coachman or chairman shall refuse to go at, or exact more for his hire than according to these rates, he shall forfeit a sum not exceeding 31 (£3.00) nor under 10s and on misbehaviour, by abusive language, or otherwise, the commissioners may revoke his licence or inflict a penalty; and on non-payment, he shall be committed to Bridewell, and kept to hard labour for thirty days.

APPENDIX 2 : Metropolitan Police Regulations for the Construction and Licensing of Hackney (Motor) Carriages, 1906

Notice to Proprietors as to conditions for obtaining a Certificate of Fitness for Motor Hackney Carriages

Carriages must be submitted for inspection in a thoroughly good condition, and no carriage will be certified fit for public use unless it is newly painted and varnished. The following conditions must also be strictly complied with :

1. Hackney carriages propelled by mechanical means, and subject to the Light Locomotives Act *(59 and 60 Vict., C. 36)* and Motor Car Act *(3 Edwd. VII., C. 36)*, must comply with the requirements of those Acts, and of the Orders of the Local Government Board made in pursuance thereof.

2. Each new type of motor car intended for licensing must be presented at New Scotland Yard for inspection. The proprietor must at the same time produce the certificate of registration, and also one from the maker stating the machinery to be safe and in every way fit for use in a public carriage.

If, on inspection, the car is approved, such approval may extend to all cars of that description, and cars of that type need not be again presented at New Scotland Yard; but may be taken to the usual passing station, provided a certificate from the maker is submitted with each car for licensing, stating that it is in every respect similar to the type already approved.

A certificate from the proprietor, stating there has been no alteration in the design of the machinery since the previous inspection and date covered by the maker's certificate, must be presented with each car submitted for renewal of licence.

Should an alteration be made, the same course may be required as for a first inspection.

Should it be deemed necessary, an expert will be employed to advise on the subject. The fee for the expert examination to be deposited by the proprietor with the Commissioner, which fee will be returned if the car is passed without alteration being required.

3. The following measurements and requirements for a hackney carriage should be adhered to:

CHASSIS

Clearance. The front axle and all the underworks of the car inside the knuckles of the steering joints (provided they are placed as near as possible to the wheels), as far back at least as the rear axle, must clear the ground at least 10in when the car is fully loaded.

The chassis wheelbase should in all cases be so proportioned that skidding or other improper movements shall be as far as possible avoided.

(NOTE. The Commissioner reserves the right, even after a car has been passed, if it is found to be apt to skid unduly, to issue a notice on the proprietor not to use, and may refuse to licence again until the defects have been remedied.)

Chassis springs. The springs must be properly hung, of sufficient strength and flexibility to meet all purposes which may be required of them. Those springs carrying the load must be attached to, or bear upon, the back axle as near to the wheels as possible. The distance between the outsides of the rear springs shall not be less than 40in. The front springs must be as wide apart as possible, but not less than 32in from outside to outside.

The centre of wheel track must not be less than 4ft 4in.

BODY (HANSOM PATTERN)

Height inside, from the top of seat cushions to the roof at the lowest part, or where the front window frames fold up toward the roof to the lowest part of the frame, must not be less than 40in.

Width inside at any point must not be less than 40in.

Width from the back squab to the nearest point of door pillars not less than 26in, and for knee space not less than 28in.

BODY (LANDAULETTE OR BROUGHAM PATTERN)

Height inside from the top of seat cushions to the roof at the lowest part must not be less than 40in.

Width between the hinge pillars or shutting pillars must not be less than 40in.

Width of door must not be less than 21in, and it must be so constructed that it opens to the fullest extent, and that it causes no inconvenience to passengers.

Where the carriage is provided with front and back seats the measurement between the front edges of cushions must not be less than 19in.

Width of front seat not less than 14in, and of back seat not less than 16in.

Steps. Where more than one is used there must be a handrail, commode rail, or other suitable means to assist passengers entering and alighting, and it must be properly and rigidly fixed.

The total over-all length of the chassis and body must in no case exceed 14ft, nor the extreme breadth be greater than 5ft 9in.

4.   Each carriage must be fitted with at least two independent brakes of sufficient strength that either of them is capable of stopping and holding the carriage under all conditions.

(NOTE. The maintenance of the brakes in perfect order is of the utmost importance, and this will at all times be insisted upon. They will at any time be subject to inspection.)

5.   Each car must be capable of being readily steered, and able to turn within a circle the diameter of which does not exceed 25ft.

6.   The steering arms, etc, to be of sufficient strength and as far as possible protected from damage by collision.

7.   The machinery should be so constructed that no undue noise or vibration is caused, and the maintenance of the carriage in this condition will be strictly enforced.

8.   Effective means must be adopted for the radiation of heat, and cooling of the parts subject to heat.

9.   All wires carrying electric current to be sufficiently insulated and placed so as to be free from danger.

10.   Tanks for petrol or other liquid fuel must be made of suitable material, properly constructed, and of sufficient strength. They should be so placed that any overflow shall not accumulate on woodwork, or where it can be readily ignited. The filling nozzle or inlet for the petrol or other liquid fuel should, where possible, be brought to the outside of the body.

11.   A horn or gong for giving due warning of the approach of the vehicle must be provided.

12.   Driving chains and sprockets to be protected by a suitable guard.

13.   Headlights of great brilliancy will not be permitted.

14.   Each carriage must have a check string or some other means for the hirer to communicate with the driver.

15.   The number of passengers which the vehicle is licensed to carry to be legibly painted on the back of the carriage outside.

16. Where acetylene or other gas is used to light the carriage, the cylinders or vessels which contain the gas, or in which it is generated, must be fixed outside in such a position as to be removed as far as possible from the danger of accidental ignition.

17. Straps with holes are to be placed on the window frames (where considered necessary), and metal or bone knobs must be fixed inside the carriage, to enable the windows to be partially closed.

18. Carriages, the floors of which are above 18in from the ground, must have suitable steps.

19. Space should be provided for the conveyance of a reasonable quantity of luggage, and some means for securing the same must be fixed.

20. The floor must be covered with rubber, coir mats, or some other suitable material.

21. No printed, written, or other matter shall appear on the inside or outside of the carriage, or be carried by way of advertisement.

22. No celluloid or xylonite fittings to be placed inside or outside, but this does not apply to the inside of accumulators.

23. There must be proper ventilation without opening the windows.

24. Some effectual means must be provided to prevent the rattling of window frames and glass.

25. A lamp must be fixed on the right or offside of the carriage, and another at the rear to provide for the illumination of the identification plate.

26. The cushions of seats, where such are provided, to be covered with leather, cloth of good quality, or other suitable material, and not stuffed with hay, straw, seaweed, or whalebone shavings. Inferior American, or a similar cloth, or any material of inferior quality, is not regarded as suitable for public carriages.

27. The doors, windows, seats, roof, springs, wheels, cushions, linings, panels, etc, and all furniture and appointments of the carriage, must be in perfect order and repair, the paint and varnish bright and in good condition, and the inside perfectly clean.

(NOTE. Though the above conditions may have been complied with, yet, if there be anything in the construction, form, or general appearance which, in the opinion of the Commissioner, renders the carriage unfit for public use, it will not be licensed.)

E. R. HENRY
The Commissioner of Police of the Metropolis

Public Carriage Office,
New Scotland Yard,
23rd March, 1906.

APPENDIX 3 : Metropolitan Police Regulations for the Construction and Licensing of Motor Cabs in London

(Amended September 1971)

Conditions of Fitness : General Construction

Every cab must comply in all respects with the requirements of any Acts and Regulations relating to motor vehicles in force at the time of licensing.

STEERING

(1) The steering wheel must be on the offside of the vehicle.

(2) The steering mechanism must be so constructed or arranged that NO overlock is possible and that the road wheels do not in any circumstances foul any part of the vehicle.

(3) The steering arms and connections must be of adequate strength and as far as possible protected from damage by collision.

BRAKE AND STEERING CONNECTIONS

Where brake and steering connections are secured with bolts or pins, the bolts or pins must be threaded and fitted with approved locking devices and they must be so placed that, when in any position other than horizontal, the head of the bolt or pin is uppermost.

TURNING CIRCLE

(1) The vehicle must be capable of being turned on either lock so as to proceed in the opposite direction without reversing between two vertical parallel planes not more than 28ft apart.

(2) The wheel turning circle kerb to kerb on either lock must not be less than 25ft in diameter.

TYRES

All tyres at normal pressure under load must be approved as having a suitable minimum circumference for correct operation of the taximeter.

BRAKES

(1) All brakes must act directly on the wheels of the vehicle.

(2) The brakes of one of the braking systems must be applied by pedal and, with the exception of the stop-light switch, no brake mechanism may operate any other separate mechanism.

(3) The pedal-operated braking system must be so designed that notwithstanding the failure of the brakes on the front or rear pair of wheels there must still be available for application, brakes on the other pair sufficient to bring the vehicle to rest within a reasonable distance.

(4) Cable connections are not permitted in the pedal-operated system and only if specially approved in the handbrake system.

SUSPENSION

(I) Every vehicle must be fitted with an efficient suspension system so designed and constructed that there is no excessive roll or pitch.

(2) Every vehicle must be so constructed or adapted that a failure of a spring, torsion bar or other similar component of the suspension system is not likely to cause the driver to lose directional control of the vehicle.

(3) When the vehicle is complete and fully equipped for service and loaded with weights placed in the correct relative positions to represent the driver and a full complement of passengers and luggage and is placed on a plane surface, it must not overturn when the plane is tilted to either side to an angle of 40° from the horizontal.

(4) If a roof rack is subsequently fitted the vehicle must be re-submitted for this test.

NOTE : (a) For the purposes of this Condition 140lb shall be deemed to represent the weight of one person and 140lb the weight of a full complement of luggage.

(b) For the purposes of conducting tests of stability the height of any stop used to prevent a wheel from slipping sideways must not be greater than two-thirds of the distance between the surface upon which the vehicle stands before it is tilted and that part of the rim of that wheel which is then nearest to such surface when the vehicle is loaded.

(c) If the vehicle is submitted with a roof rack half the luggage is to be on the roof.

BOLTS AND NUTS

All moving parts and parts subject to severe vibration connected by bolts or studs and nuts must be fitted with an approved locking device.

FUEL TANKS

(1) Fuel tanks must not be placed under the bonnet and must be adequately protected from damage by collision.

(2) All fuel tanks and all apparatus supplying fuel to the engine must be so placed or shielded that no fuel overflowing or leaking therefrom can fall or accumulate upon any part or fitting where it is capable of being readily ignited or can fall into any receptacle where it might accumulate.

(3) The filling points for all fuel tanks must be accessible only from the outside of the vehicle and filler caps must be so designed and constructed that they cannot be dislodged by accidental operation.

(4) A device must be provided by means of which the supply of fuel to the engine may be immediately cut off. Its situation together with the means of operation and 'off' position must be clearly marked on the outside of the vehicle. In the case of a petrol engine, the device must be visible and readily accessible at all times from outside the vehicle.

INTERIOR LIGHTING

Adequate lighting must be provided for the passengers' compartment and must be capable of being controlled by passengers and driver. Adequate lighting must be provided in the driver's compartment.

ELECTRICAL EQUIPMENT

(1) All electrical leads and cables must be adequately insulated and where liable to be affected by exposure to water, petrol or oil, must be adequately protected.

(2) All electrical circuits must be protected by suitable fuses.

(3) Batteries must be so placed and protected that they cannot be a source of danger.

FIRE APPLIANCES

An appliance for extinguishing fire must be carried in such a position as to be readily available for use and such appliance must comply with the requirements relating to fire extinguishing appliances for use on public service vehicles.

EXHAUST PIPE

The exhaust pipe must be so fitted or shielded that no inflammable material can fall or be thrown upon it from any other part of the vehicle and that it is not likely to cause a fire through proximity to any inflammable material on the vehicle. The outlet must be placed at the rear of the vehicle on the off-side and in such a position as to prevent fumes from entering the vehicle.

BODY

(1) The body must be of the fixed-head type with a partially glazed partition separating the passenger from the driver.

(2) (a) Outside dimensions:
   (i) The overall width of the vehicle exclusive of driving mirrors must not exceed 5ft 9in.
   (ii) The overall length must not exceed 15ft.
   (b) Inside dimensions of passengers' compartment:
   (i) The vertical distance between the point of maximum deflection of the seat cushion when a passenger is seated to the roof immediately above that point must not be less than 38in.
   (ii) The width across the rear seat cushion must not be less than 42in.

(3) Any curvature of the floor of the passengers' compartment must be continuous and must not exceed $\frac{3}{4}$in at the partition and 2in at the base of the rear seat when measured between the centre line and the sills.

(4) The door and doorway must be so constructed as to permit of an unrestricted opening across the doorway of at least 21in when the door is opened to its normal limit.

(5) The height of the doorway from the top of the sill must not be less than 47in.

(6) Where a boot-lid is fitted it must be hinged at the top.

STEPS

(I) The top of the tread of the lowest step for any entrance, or where there is no step the floor level itself at the entrance, must not be more than 15in above the ground when the vehicle is unladen.

(2) All steps, or where there are no steps the outer edge of the floor at each entrance, must be fitted with non-slip treads.

PASSENGERS' SEATS

(1) The measurements from the upholstery at the back to the front edge of the seat must not be less than 16in in the case of the back seat and 14in in the case of the front seat.

(2) The width of each front seat must not be less than 16in.

(3) The vertical distance between the highest point of the undeflected seat cushion and the top of the floor covering must not be less than 14in.

(4) Where seats are placed facing each other there must be a clear space of 19in between any part of the front of a seat and any part of any other seat which faces it. This measurement may be reduced to 17in provided adequate foot room is maintained at floor level. Where all seats are placed facing to the front of the vehicle there must be a clear space of at least 26in in front of every part of each seat squab.

(5) Front seats must be so arranged as to rise automatically when not in use. They must be symmetrically placed and at least 1½in apart. When not in use, front seats must not obstruct doorways.

(6) Suitable means must be provided to assist persons to rise from the rear seat.

DRIVER'S COMPARTMENT

(1) The driver's compartment must be so designed that the driver has adequate room, can easily reach and quickly operate the controls and give hand signals on the offside of the vehicle.

(2) The controls must be so placed as to allow reasonable access to the driver's seat and, when centrally placed, must be properly protected from contact with luggage.

(3) The driver's seat must be designed to accommodate the driver only.

(4) An offside door must be fitted to the driver's compartment.

(5) The driver's forward and rear visibility and wiping of the windscreen must be in accordance with the Society of Motor Manufacturers' & Traders' Standard No 5 'Code of Recommended Practice for Driving Vision'.

(6) The vehicle must be fitted with adequate devices for demisting,

defrosting and washing the windscreen and with a sun visor adjustable by the driver.

(7) Direction indicators of an approved type must be fitted.

(8) Every cab must be provided with an approved means of communication between the passenger and the driver. When a sliding window is fitted at the rear of the driver's compartment, the maximum width of the opening must not exceed 4½in.

WINDOWS

(1) Windows must be provided at the sides and at the rear.

(2) Passenger door windows must be capable of being opened easily by passengers.

HEATING

An adequate heating system must be fitted for the driver and passengers and means provided for independent control by the driver and passengers.

GLASS

The windscreen and all windows and glass partions must be toughened glass in accordance with the latest British Standard at the time of approval.

DOOR FITTINGS

(1) Passengers' doors must be capable of being readily opened from inside and outside the vehicle by one operation of the locking mechanism.

(2) Double catches of approved type must be fitted to all doors.

FARE TABLE FRAME AND NUMBER PLATE

A frame must be provided for the fare table and interior number plate and fitted in an approved position. The words 'The number of this cab is —' are to be shown above the position for the interior number plate.

FLOOR COVERING

The flooring of the passengers' compartment must be covered with non-slip material which can easily be cleaned.

LUGGAGE

(1) Provision must be made for carrying luggage and an efficient method of securing it must be provided.

(2) If it is intended to carry luggage on the roof, a fixed roof-guard rail of approved type must be fitted.

HORN

A deep-toned horn of approved pattern must be fitted.

TAXIMETER

A taximeter of an approved type must be fitted in an approved position.

'TAXI' SIGNS

A 'Taxi' sign of approved pattern, clearly visible both by day and by night when the cab is not hired, must be fitted.

RADIO APPARATUS

Where apparatus for the operation of a two-way radio system is fitted to a cab, no part of the apparatus may be fixed in the passengers' compartment.

FITTINGS

No fittings other than those approved may be attached to or carried upon the inside or outside of the cab.

REGISTRATION MARK

Letters and figures must be white on a black background, or comply with regulation 7a, of the Road Vehicles (Registration & Licensing) (Amendment) (No 2) Regulations 1967, relating to reflex-reflecting plates.

ADVERTISEMENTS

No printed, written or other matter by way of advertisements may appear on the outside of the cab. Suitable advertisements may be allowed on the inside of cabs, subject to the approval of the Assistant Commissioner.

MAINTENANCE

Cabs, including all fittings, etc, must be well maintained and kept clean and in good working order. The vehicles will at all times be subject to test and inspection and should it be found that a cab is not being properly maintained or that any part or fitting is not in good working order, a notice will be served on the owner prohibiting him from using the vehicle until the defect has been remedied.

CERTIFICATE OF INSURANCE AND FORM OF HOLDER

A current certificate of insurance as required by any Acts or Regulations relating to motor vehicles, with an addition certifying also that the policy to which the certificate relates complies with the requirements of the London Cab Order, 1934, must be carried in a holder securely affixed to the cab in an approved position.

K

APPENDIX 4 : Taxi Fares (by distance), 1900-1971

NOTE: The initial charge shows the rate payable for the first mile; often there was a lower initial charge, such as 6d for the first ⅔rds of a mile, but to show relative charges over the whole period this figure has been scaled up to the rate payable for one complete mile.

Date	Initial charge	Additional charge (per mile)	Extras (per passenger above two)	(per piece of luggage)
1900-1917 (horse cab)	6d	6d	6d	2d
1907-1917 (motor cab)	8d	8d	6d	2d
1917-1920	1s 2d	8d	6d	2d
1920-1927	1s	1s	9d	3d
1927-1933	9d	9d	6d	3d
1933-1951	1s	9d	6d	3d
1951-1959	1s 9d	1s 3d	6d*	3d
1959-1963	2s 3d	1s 3d	6d*	3d
1963-1968	2s 8d	1s 8d	6d*	3d
1968-1970	2s 10½d	1s 10½d	6d*	3d
Sept. 1970	6d surcharge on all hirings			
Feb. 1971 to date (decimal)	20p	12p	3p*	3p

* Since 1957 this charge has applied to all passengers above one.

APPENDIX 5 : Specifications of Representative Taxicabs

Make and Model	*Date of Introduction*	*Number of Cylinders*	*Bore and Stroke*	*Cubic Capacity*	*Number of Forward Speeds*	*Wheelbase*	*Overall Length*
Rational 10hp	1905	2	110 × 120mm	2,090cc	2	6ft 6in	
Unic 10/12hp	1906	2	102 × 110mm	1,750cc	3	8ft 4$\frac{1}{2}$in	11ft 9in
Unic 12/14hp	1908	4	75 × 110mm	1,944cc	3	8ft 4$\frac{1}{2}$in	11ft 9in
Renault 7/9hp	1907	2	81 × 120mm	1,260cc	3	8ft 4in	11ft 6$\frac{1}{2}$in
Napier 10hp	1909	2	82.5 × 127mm	1,375cc	3	8ft 0in	12ft 0in
Belsize 14/16hp	1912	4	93 × 120mm	3,260cc	4	8ft 1$\frac{1}{2}$in	12ft 0in
Charron 15.9hp	1912	4	80 × 120mm	2,413cc	3	9ft 0in	12ft 8in
Beardmore 15.6hp	1919	4	79 × 120mm	2,409cc	4	8ft 6in	11ft 7$\frac{1}{4}$in
Fiat Tipo 1T	1920	4	70 × 120mm	1,846cc		8ft 11$\frac{7}{8}$in	12ft 7$\frac{3}{8}$in
Citroen 11.4hp	1923	4	68 × 100mm	1,453cc	3	8ft 1$\frac{7}{8}$in	11ft 6in
Hayes 15.9hp	1924	4	80 × 120mm	2,413cc	3	8ft 5$\frac{1}{2}$in	11ft 9in
Yellow Cab 18.3hp	1924	4	86 × 127mm	3,050cc	3	8ft 3in	11ft 8in
Morris Commercial International	1929	4	80 × 125mm	2,513cc	4	9ft 0in	12ft 8in
Beardmore Hyper	1929	4	72 × 120mm	1,954cc	4	9ft 0in	12ft 9in
Austin Twelve Four	1930	4	72 × 114.5mm	1,861cc	4	9ft 4in	13ft 6in
Unic KF1	1930	4	72.8 × 120mm	1,998cc	4	9ft 6in	13ft 7in
Morris Commercial Junior Six	1934	6	63.5 × 102mm	1,938cc	4	9ft 0in	13ft 10in
Wolseley Oxford	1946	4	75 × 102mm	1,802cc	4	8ft 11$\frac{1}{2}$in	13ft 11$\frac{1}{2}$in
Austin FX3	1948	4	79.4 × 111.1mm	2,199cc	4	9ft 2$\frac{5}{8}$in	14ft 5$\frac{1}{4}$in
Beardmore Mark VII	1954	4	79.37 × 76.2mm	1,508cc	4	8ft 8in	13ft 10$\frac{1}{2}$in
Beardmore Mark VIID	1958	4	76.2 × 88.9mm	1,628cc			
Austin FX4D	1958	4	82.5 × 101.6mm	2,178cc	4	9ft 2$\frac{5}{8}$in	15ft 0$\frac{1}{2}$in
Austin FX4 (petrol)	1962	4	79.4 × 111.1mm	2,199cc			
Winchester diesel	1963	4	76.2 × 88.9mm	1,628cc	4	8ft 10in	14ft 9in
Winchester petrol	1965	4	80.97 × 72.82mm	1,499cc			
Metrocab	1970	4	79.5 × 88.9mm	1,760cc	4	8ft 4in	13ft 6in
Austin FX4D	1971	4	89 × 101.6mm	2,520cc	4	9ft 2$\frac{5}{8}$in	15ft 0$\frac{1}{2}$in

BIBLIOGRAPHY

Armstrong, A., *Taxi* (Hodder & Stoughton, 1930)
Buckland, Robert, *Share My Taxi* (Michael Joseph, 1968)
Gilbey, Sir Walter, *Early Carriages and Roads* (Vinton, 1903)
Knight, Charles, *Knight's London* (Charles Knight, 1842)
Levinson, Maurice, *Taxi* (Secker & Warburg, 1963)
Moore, H. C., *Omnibuses and Cabs* (Chapman & Hall, 1902)
Ten Thousand Hackney Coach Fares (T. Hughes, 1805)

Apart from these books, the author has consulted innumerable issues of *The Commercial Motor*, *Motor Traction*, *Motor Transport* and *Steering Wheel*, together with occasional references in *Autocar*, *The Automotor Journal*, *Country Life* and *Road and Track*.

ACKNOWLEDGEMENTS

The author offers grateful thanks to the following for valuable help in many ways:

Eric Bellamy, Librarian of the Montagu Motor Museum
Alan Broughton
Jack C. Cohen
V. R. Cook, managing director, W. H. Cook & Sons Ltd
K. E. Drummond, managing director, Winchester Automobiles (West End) Ltd
Mrs Pamela Egan
Paul Hermon
Patrick Hickman-Robertson
Arthur Ingram
T. G. C. Knowlys
Dr George Morey, BBC News Information Service
Miss Pauline Noakes, BBC News Information Service
Hans-Otto Neubauer
R. C. H. Overton, director, Mann & Overton Ltd
R. Perkins
Norman Richards, Educational Department, Transport & General Workers' Union
Michael Sedgwick
F. Skelton
D. J. Southwell, director, Mann & Overton Ltd
G. W. Trotter, managing director, London General Cab Co Ltd

Photographs are acknowledged in the list on pages 7 and 8, but the author and publisher would like to thank Messrs Chapman & Hall Ltd for permission to reproduce the line drawings on pages 21, 25, 27, 29, 30, 33, 37 and 41, the Editor of *Punch* for those on pages 43, 67 and 77, and the Editor of *Autocar* for that on page 149. Also William Heineman Ltd for permission to reproduce the extract on pages 22-3.

INDEX

(NOTE: page numbers in italics refer to illustrations)

178   INDEX